Conduct

CONSPIRACY CORRUPTION COURAGE

Norton Doran

ISBN: 1499100361
ISBN 13: 9781499100365
Library of Congress Control Number: 2014907368
CreateSpace Independent Publishing Platform
North Charleston, South Carolina
http://nortonbdoran.com

con·duct (Kan'dukt') n

1 management; 2 behavior

Do all the good you can
By all the means you can
In all the ways you can
In all the places you can
At all the times you can
To all the people you can
As long as you ever can

"Rule of Conduct"
JOHN WESLEY (1703 – 1791)

CONTENTS

PROLOGUE

As we all move through life, we will be part of creating, joining, or ending a myriad of situations that are a mix of chance and plans. How we benefit or suffer from these encounters depends largely on *if* we can predict them or not, and then deal with them. When the situation is upon us, we will be at some point on the situation line or curve. This line or curve can go up if the situation is in our favor, or down if the situation is not in our favor. We will be somewhere between the beginning and the end. An example of a rising curve might be that of some good information about an investment opportunity where we buy in, ride the upward trend, pick a point of the trend to sell out, and pocket a profit. An example of a situational line going down might be that of an armed burglar crashing through your window in the middle of the night. You might win or you might lose. It does not matter... it is going to end quickly and will not be good. There was no advance planning for *that* encounter. The situation was "game on" from start to finish and went fast.

Here is a presentation of various influences that can shape your life as you proceed into the future. How you *Conduct* yourself in dealing with these influences or "forces," will have consequences that can include pleasure, profit, prestige, and power. Of course, the results could just as easily go badly leaving you a broken, penniless person with one eye, confined to a wheelchair. I hope that the counsel I offer in this paper will give you some ideas that will keep you on a rising curve, or at least, give you some information about what you might have to deal with. Plan to chuckle or laugh now and then... intensity will come in due time.

Probably the hardest part of any advice is convincing people that obstacles, threats, and invisible forces really *are* "out there" to hinder, obscure, or obliterate their intensions, progress and accomplishments. The effort becomes even more difficult when I try to impress upon folks how the seemingly oddest people who are presumed to be helping and supporting them, are actually saying one thing and *doing* quite another... in-other-words, out to "get them." Of course, if you are one of those "teenager types" who already know everything, then I should send you back to mommy, pals, handlers, or whatever.

The main message here is simple – There is REAL opportunity to achieve success for the person who is willing to give the sweat and time required. Many people are available who have your best interests at heart and are willing to help you. A great number of successful people are standing by to help you join their ranks. They know, and so will you, that the view from the top is a good view. A few of us getting older actually have to grow up and accept some responsibility... hopefully earlier than later. So, put on your smile with a positive attitude and go for it..

> *The really important thing is not to live, but to live well. And to live well meant, along with more enjoyable things in life, to live according to your principles.*
>
> - Socrates (c. 469 BC – 399 BC)

CHAPTER 1

CONDUCT

It is nice to be here for you. Some time soon, I imagine you all will be generating ideas and products that other folks want and/or need, and being substantially compensated for the effort. I offer you my sincere support and blessing for all the time and energy you will spend. For some, the endeavor will be the simple and a proverbial "walk in the park." For most, it will be a long, tough climb. It will be a march of expense, disappointment, pain and exposure. You will be exposed to people who could care less about how you feel or what you think. Your well-being will matter to few, if anyone at all.

Employment and the fun of working for money, from which you will buy your living, is "out there" - but *when* you find it, may take some serious time.

Here in the second quarter of 2014, many people in government and big corporations are working overtime to make sure a substantial portion of the private sector of the American workforce suffers. Worse, through a plethora of federal agencies, with little or no oversight... the politicians and bureaucrats inside the beltway are dreaming up more and more ways to slow down progress in America, thereby limiting profits to people and groups who work hard, try to get ahead, and help others in the process through their entrepreneurship.

I hope that you can take from my words some meaningful information to deal with the forces you will encounter. I will try to impart some wisdom that will keep you cheerful, attentive and focused, as well as going forth with positive expectations. I want to cover a lot of material and make it worth your while.

For me, trying to say something not already said by others is a difficult task. With all the books, magazines, songs and speeches that have been written over the centuries; all the plays, movies, skits, stage acts, television shows, catchy political rhetoric and more; those who have had the help of legions of writers preparing material; and the daily conversation of those trying to make a point - it seems as if "all has been said." However, now it is my turn. I will probably say something we have heard before because it makes the point. I will try to give proper credit.

This paper is about CONDUCT – *our* Conduct in various forums as I see it. Conduct is a style of life that is meaningless to some, important to others, and a science of experience to few.

Conduct

Rendering opinions on any subject is dangerous, so strap in. This might get bumpy.

Never discourage anyone who continually makes progress... no matter how slow.

- Plato (c. 427 BC – 347 BC)

CHAPTER 2

RULES

One of the reason's we can function with any dignity is simply because we have laws, rules and regulations creating a framework within which to Conduct ourselves. The first of two sets are the written rules - the ones telling us where to park a car or pay property taxes. Second are the implied rules - like proper behavior in day-to-day living – as in *etiquette*.

We have a couple other laws as well – natural and fabricated. The natural laws, of course, pertain to everything that man cannot control, such as planetary movement, gemstone hardness and so on. I would almost be willing to bet *your* life there are bureaucrats trying to regulate the planets. The fabricated laws fall into two more categories – good and bad!

On a more serious note, our laws here in the United States should be Constitutional, whereby we are governed by a specific set of guidelines as a Republic for the common good of all. Unfortunately, the ink of the founding fathers' signatures was barely dry before the Constitution came under attack from people who wanted a monarchy, or even anarchy. Since long ago, our Constitution has been under attack by the very politicians who have sworn to *uphold* the directions set forth in that document. Whether you do, or do not agree with the way law and politics have evolved... the verifiable fact remains - most laws coming out of the beltway (our nation's capital) have penalized the private sector of the work force to the benefit of political cronies and others not deserving of such favor. Worse, the federal laws have grossly overstepped the boundaries of the Constitution with the complicity of the president and the Congress, completely disregarding the common productive citizen who made it all possible in the first place.

Moving on to the astonishing and illegal Administrative Law we are burdened with, we find numerous alphabet agencies such as EPA (Environmental Protection Agency), DHS (Department of Homeland Security), DOE (Department of Education), and many more. Then, we have several enforcement agencies like FBI (Federal Bureau of Investigation), DEA (Drug Enforcement Agency) and more of those also. Add to that, all the government *spooks* (secret agents) from NSA (National Security Agency), CIA (Central Intelligence Agency) and plenty more... making the existence of a common citizen akin to navigating in a minefield. You are probably familiar with some of the state and local laws, rules and regulations covering everything from murder to property-line setback. Good luck trying to drill an oil well or dig a mine. Most of the manufacturing that has left the U.S. did so because of all the burdensome laws, rules and regulations. The government-mandated compliance has made industrial manufacturing costs so high, and the rewards so low, we are left with massive unemployment and poverty – all paid for, of course, by those who still have a job. The ability of business and industry to manage their own development by rightfully expecting employees to accept direction and responsibility has been replaced by disinterested third-party regulators looking for an excuse to punish those companies. There is plenty of rotten and illegal Statutory and Common Law as well. Remember this - *the government cannot give away anything it has not taken from someone else.*

As you move through life in your search for success and a wonderful future, you will be crossing paths, interfacing, meeting, and working with many people. It will be good experience and contribute to your Character. Therefore, if you get the urge to say, or do, something stupid, be sure it is reversible.

It seems as if many people are always trying to impress some thought or Conduct upon other people – maybe hoping to garner support for their own thoughts or create some sort of so-called "legacy," as in changing existing rules or constructing a memorial to some person or cause. Sometimes the proposals are good, sometimes not. You may have to get involved sooner or later if the changes sought impact you.

All that said, employment and success is still "out there." If your chips are down and your cards not good, you can always drive a truck or work for the government. I will take the truck. I prefer not be thought of by anyone as I think of a few non-producers who are milking the government tit.

Here is a little jingle - Things you have done
                               Things you say
                               When you are gone
                               They are here to stay.

Maybe this is a good time to hear the important words of another good person –

People may not remember exactly what you did, or what you said, but they will always remember how you made them feel.
                              – Maya Angelou (1928 – 2014)

CHAPTER 3

CHARACTER

Character is the core of your soul. It is your armor that should remain shining at all times. It is the quality with which you represent yourself.

Character goes two ways, just like those rules... good and bad. There is a gray area, but it is subjective.

If you are an individual of Good Character, opportunities are available to you that are not available to others. People of Good Character can generally be trusted to follow through on commitments in a timely fashion, present meaningful information and ideas, offer helpful reflections of ideas presented by others and are pleasant people to be near. They are this way for many reasons, and a few of those reasons might be because they are following tenets set forth Biblically and intellectually – as in the Ten Commandments

(Ex. 20: 3 – 17), and the Golden Rule (Matt. 7:12), or relying on suggestions by friends, family and philosophers who contribute positive and interesting thoughts toward dealing with people and situations.

People of Bad Character absolutely cannot be trusted and carry costly baggage. They can be liars, cheats, thieves, murderers, and so on. Murder is horrible, but as Character flaws go, being a liar seems to be the granddaddy of them all since so many people are liars. A little white lie or a big black lie… does not matter. Once the lying starts, it is difficult to slow it down. Liars will lie about everything. They lie, and swear to God they are telling the truth. They will lie for other liars and lie *about* other people. I have heard it said that everybody lies. Hmmm… people with agendas and conspiracies or something to hide? Maybe deflecting nosy questions gets a pass (?).

These bad people will come sniffing around looking for a weak and/or gullible person on who to Conduct their dirty deeds… cheating at cards, short-changing transactions, molesting your kids, damaging your property, robbing, raping – you name it. They are comprised of a dark and devious group. If someone appears questionable to you, steer clear… it costs nothing. Oh yeah, they will also swear on their mother's grave.

I suppose *accidental* liars get a pass, of sorts. These poor folks believe and repeat bad information they truly think is correct. The Character problems arise when they defend their position after having been called on it.

If there is a Gray Character, it will be in the eyes of the observer. You may never know that you, yourself, might fall into this group… or why you are thought of in this fashion. However, experience has taught me that you will usually know if there is a problem. People of Gray Character are not bad people... they just have an attribute that gives someone else cause for concern.

If someone refers to you as a nice person, "*but....*," that someone is probably suggesting you have a flaw. They remember something you did or said and they think it has tarnished your armor. It is best to try to find out what or why and take some sort of action – usually an apology goes a long way if they were offended sometime in the past. Beyond that, good luck.

Some poor well-meaning individual may have had unpaid debts that cost jail time. He or she has not lied to you or injured any-one, fully admitted to some shortcomings and does excellent yard work. Do you want that person to marry your kid or come over for Christmas dinner? Beats me – it might be Gray Character.

Character has a lot to do with your poise, presence, speech and demeanor. If you are out in public, or show up at a job interview with a smile, coat, tie, polished shoes, groomed hair, beard, and speaking proper English, you will probably go a lot further than someone who shows up wearing worn out jeans, tee shirt, stooped shoulders, greasy hair, and speaking with a phony, twang drawl.

Henry Clay (1777 – 1852) was a very important person who served this country in the Congress as both Senator and Representative during the years of 1806 – 1852. He had a few words about Character from which we may benefit – *Of all the properties which belong to honorable men, not one is so highly prized as that of character.*

Conduct and Character – they go together.

CHAPTER 4

POLITICS, POWER & AGENDAS

You may have heard an old worn out adage, "Never talk about politics, religion or sex." Well, I have a news flash for you. Those are probably the most important topics you may ever discuss. Eventually, people near each other will get around to identifying their ideology, if for no other reason than to start an argument. Most of us will test others to see if we are in a "safe" place. A fast track out the door and into the unemployment line might result from declaring someone corrupt, or some program unconstitutional, or maybe stating how horrible some so-called religion is, and of course alluding to lust or sexual preference of another person. Being right or wrong does not matter. You will meet the wall of power and perception, and that wall belongs to the *other guy*.

Saying nothing at all is the safe bet. It might be boring, but it's safe. An awful lot of people talk too much, and I can give first-hand testimony on that. Unfortunately, saying almost anything and being honest and right, might not be *politically correct.* It will set the stage for liars and others who can be dangerous.

Having science, empirical data and the associated logic to go with any subject can be dangerous – literally. Drawing attention to someone's behavior might be funny for some and deadly for others. You just do not know until you have been in their "mix" for some time. Probably some of the best examples of being dangerously right would be in the arena of government crime and corruption. After all, what is a "whistleblower?" A small amount of basic research will reveal that most whistleblowers who are trying to expose the Three-C's (Crime, Corruption & Cover-up) generally end up on a distressing and difficult road. Our federal infrastructure is so corrupt, there are few, *if any*, people who can be trusted in dealing with evidence of criminal Conduct in federal circles (or maybe any circles, for that matter). Many government people causing trouble are linked to other government people and the cover-up runs all the way to the White House. The mode of operation is simple – deny it, cover it up and go after the whistle-blowing good guy.

The United States has just about completed the transition from a Republic to some bastardization of Communism. Trying to describe how this is, how it has gotten to be this way, and why anyone would want it, is beyond the scope of this paper, but the politicians are all a bunch of polished liars. Why would they stand in front of a nation, promise to uphold the Constitution, and then do precisely the opposite? Corruption is a good place to start. In political circles, I think they call that "going along to get along."

I'll give you my idea of how the *road-to-ruin* got started, shortly.

Let's take a stroll through a little history and see what some other folks thought about politics...

> *Practical politics consists in ignoring facts.*
>> Henry Adams, son of Charles Adams,
>> grandson of John Quincy Adams, and
>> great-grandson of John Adams (c. 1906)

> *Politics is perhaps the only profession for which no preparation is thought necessary.*
>> Robert Louis Stevenson (1902)

At the present time, the *absolute* power center of the world seems to be Washington, DC. Also in this center of activity is a very concentrated control of vast wealth. Money is power and trumps political rank. For a large part of the past and present, politicians do what well-moneyed manipulators (handlers) instruct. Brussels, Belgium is an important power-center as well.

Lord Acton, in a letter to Mandell Creighton, April 5, 1887, summed it up this way –
> *Power tends to corrupt and absolute power corrupts absolutely. Great men are almost always bad men, even when they exercise influence and not authority: still more when you superadd the tendency or the certainty of corruption by authority.* (The use of the word *superadd* is rare, but generally, it is taken to mean something on the order of *make greater* or *intensify*)

This power "thing" is a lot worse and messier than most folks know, or care to admit. You see, by having all the power, "they" make all the rules and decide which one to apply to you and when to enforce it. "They" reserve to themselves all the self-created administrations to deal with all matters of business… and most of your life, as well. "They" is *central* government – federal thugs.

There are numerous federal people trying to do an excellent job for you. These folks try very hard to resolve your issue and for the most part, do a fine job. *The people working in Research and Development Labs, most military schools, troops of all kind, and surely a few others, can consider themselves exempt from my criticism.* My contention is primarily with the elected, appointed, chosen and hired group - bureaucrats. The problems start when the first or second level of responsibility cannot resolve your issue. More than one poor slob has spent huge quantities of time, money and tears dealing with government people who do not or will not "deal."

If you find yourself in the crosshairs of one of the alphabet agencies, life can be a hard lesson indeed. We are in a total surveillance state, and soon, a police state. With all the cameras in use on the street, in the buildings, in transportation, in the air with drones, all telephone and internet use illegally tapped and stored - just about all human activity here in the U.S. is monitored, recorded and stored. Other countries have the same problem, but ours is unique because of the corrupt politicians and judges who are willing to scrap our Constitution and declare you guilty by accusation or association until proven innocent. See the problem? If someone wants you out of his or her way, an anonymous phone call to some "agency" can put you in hell.

Conduct

I am sure all the surveillance has helped "law enforcement" with some issues. Problem is, do we really need it all? What about your cell phone being used as a remote and secret microphone for the arbitrary amusement of some third-party clown to listen in and see if your conversation can be deemed *suspicious* and subsequently wreck your life? Your communications about any investments, development of new ideas, forecasts of future issues and expecta-tions are all in the hands of others just itching to cash in or put you in jail. Folks, it sure looks as if the REAL criminals are in our government and trying VERY hard to criminalize YOUR behavior. Jolly good Conduct by the government spooks, *isn't* it?

I suppose some of you will end up as G-men or spooks. Let me know so I can hide from you.

Going on, the problems can get worse. What if you have a dispute with a government policy, procedure, ruling or action... now what? This can get sticky because some of the people who are supposed to be helping you are intentionally causing problems. If you think of an arrogant, territorial, agenda-driven robot, you might be real close. It is *Politics and Agendas*, folks. The road to hell can end up as an expensive crash.

I do not mean to overburden you with disparaging news, but this is how the politics and agendas are going. There really is fun and profit available. Conduct yourself properly and doors will open.

Meanwhile, here you are with a problem in hand that only your government can resolve, and you are getting lack of cooperation and outright interference. Now it gets messy. Your issue most certainly has some sort of time limit, if not a financial limit, and the machine of government has slowed, stopped or obstructed any progress. Not good. Your lawyers are taking your money and telling you not to fight city hall. At home, your family and property may be at risk, everyone is in tears wondering how and why this is happening, and the clock is running out. Now desperation sets in. Every path around the blockage is illegal – on purpose.

Taking these matters into your own hands will include dangerous possibilities such as bribing, threatening, bombing, mercenaries, assassinations and any other tactic you can dream up. Begging seldom works for anything. It would seem at this point, that the only new issues are *how high the cost is, and how high is the risk?* This can be answered by determining how badly you want your result. At this point, negotiations with *anyone* are pretty-much out of the question. It is in your best interest to be as pleasant as possible and keep your trap shut during these trying times.

Never forget corruption and remember all those surveillance cameras. These days, all conduct is monitored, cataloged, and stored somewhere. See any problem here? The surveillance might provide information of a cover-up or show a crime such as rape, robbery or murder, but the camera only *records* the deed, does not *prevent* it. Eventually, someone will come along and write a report leaving the injured parties weeping, wondering, and hoping for some sort of answer. My, my, my…

Your issue is where the going gets a little more dicey. You have gone around and around and seemingly exhausted all hopes of resolution at great expense of time, money and emotion.

Conduct

Now it is time for revenge. Now it is time to weigh the options of that satisfaction. With the Bill of Rights jammed *in the trash* can, the United States Constitution crammed *into the trash* as well, and corrupt politicians and judges behind it all, you have to decide if you have the stomach for the next step... *if* you are willing to do it and/or can find the right people to help you accomplish your end.

The government has all the cards. They have the corruption and cover-up ability. Do not underestimate the use of that pesky camera to see who is doing what, in *their* yard. So, it seemingly boils down to all that surveillance being a tool to protect *their* interests... and go after anyone who tries to interfere.

They also have a few other tools... like, all the money in the world, thousands of agents watching your every step, and a law-enforcement machine to crush anyone who dares to challenge them. These people are serious, folks. They operate with total impunity... while using *your* money, of course.

Some people die from the oddest causes... or disappear without a trace.

It is politics and agendas folks... politics and agendas...

You've heard it said before, "Desperate situations call for desperate measures." Your Conduct at this point will not only impact *your* future, but those around you as well.

> *It is inaccurate to say that I hate everything. I am strongly in favor of common sense, common honesty, and common decency. This makes me forever ineligible for public office.*
> - H. L. Mencken (1880 – 1956)

CHAPTER 5

RELIGION

Yeah, I know… hot-button territory here.

We all have a past. If you have come from a past where love and education were important, you might have an upper hand in the overall scheme of things. If you come from a past where your parents taught you the Golden Rule and maybe the Ten Commandments and maybe even something about Jesus… you might have something of value to share with the rest of the world. If your family regularly attended church, you attended Sunday school, and you are fortunate enough to come through life with a well-founded Christian ethic, you are probably cheerful, intelligent and happy. Perhaps you figured all this out completely on your own with no outside influences. The point I am trying get across is simply this - good grounding invests us with good Conduct – for the most part.

It generally means I can feel safe, if not outright protected, in your company. This is true for several reasons. I have spent years working around and studying folks trying to become a Christian. Now, at least, I know what REAL *proper* Conduct *should* be. I also know that *people do, indeed, change.* Oh... what kind of Christian? Let's go with the Full Gospel variety.

Anyone can come from *any kind of a background* that might have been riddled with all kinds of loveless bad behavior creating a bad environment for rearing children - split parents, no parents, abuses of all manner, fat, stupid, dirty, short on respect for others and *really* short on respect for themselves. That all can go away when *you* decide to make a change. *You* are the only person who can lose weight, get a haircut, take a bath, sweeten your attitude and so on. There are others willing to help with direction, money and the ever-important education to steer your change. My hope is that you do it all *and* choose to become a well-grounded Christian. Then other people observing will see Conduct illustrating that even though we may not know each other personally, we treat each other as brothers and sisters - literally. Our area becomes a safe zone... an area where we know the stakes are high and struggle is imminent, but we will stand shoulder-to-shoulder looking out for anyone who needs our help. I also know we will lock arms and defend our turf when we are threatened, and God knows there is a great deal of threatening going on.

In ours and other countries, there is plenty of killing, maiming, and misery... all to make people think and act like some group of "other" people. *Think Islam.* It is time to worry, folks. That faction of people doing the killing are serious and they are *here* to suppress and rule *you* with their brand of beliefs. It will not matter what your political or religious bend is. You can even be an atheist. That will not matter either. According to them, you need to be crushed into submission and converted... or killed. They routinely kill and maim their own. Do you see a message here?!

As Senate Chaplain Reverend Peter Marshall offered in prayer at the opening of session, April 18, 1947 – *Give us clear vision that we may know where to stand and what to stand for – because unless we stand for something, we shall fall for anything.*

I guess that beautiful prayer fell on the ears of disinterested, agenda-driven politicians who had no faith of any kind and upon hearing it, chose to ignore it. Conduct well known to their predecessors and successors, huh?

I am painfully aware of the 44th president Barack Obama (1961 -) currently occupying the White House having made an eloquent 'Call to Renewal' address where, about mid-way through that speech, June 28, 2006, he declared, *Whatever we once were, we are no longer a Christian nation – at least, not just.* He preceded and succeeded that statement with polished cover by lumping non-Christian and quasi-Christian information together, disregarding, if not denigrating, what our Founding Fathers believed and hoped to hand down to us. Remember, this same fellow, on two occasions has referred to his *muslim*[1] "faith." *I definitely do not agree that we are no longer a Christian nation,* and that statement opens the field for serious conflict. I can tell you this – when it comes to offending and insulting... *that* comment hit the jackpot – especially considering the source (See addendum). Only willing participants, complicit in that end, would suggest that we are *not* a Christian nation, and work toward the demise of Christianity.

Islam is no religion... never was, never will be. It is political ideology masquerading and being promoted as "religion." When

1 Lower case intentional

is the last time you saw any "religion" or "faith" based on hate, destruction, pain, and murder? That is Islam. Get real folks! You are being played like a wooden whistle to promote abuse and control... of YOU! Perhaps a little *research* into the past about **Islamic aggression** and wars will shed some light on all this.

The Documents to guide this nation that were composed by the founding fathers... all the supporting books, papers and speeches... the personal Conduct of those who wrote and acted for the creation of this nation... and the wonderful men and women who gave up their fortunes, limbs and lives, to build this nation... ALL had deep *Christian* beliefs and ethics. Who could have guessed at all the human garbage that would come along after them?

Here is a worthy quote by one of the important people who made this Republic possible...

I Pray Heaven to Bestow The Best of Blessing on this house, and on All that shall hereafter Inhabit it. May none but Honest and Wise Men ever rule under This Roof! These powerful words were written by our second President JOHN ADAMS (1735 – 1826), in a letter to his wife Abigail, November 2, 1800, the day after he moved into the White House.

I cannot turn this portion of my paper covering this important subject into a complete study and historical detail of our Christian foundation, but I can tell you that many liars purporting to be "of faith" and "acting in our best interest" have hijacked our heritage. To select an actual time and event on when our Free and Wonderful Republic started *seriously plummeting under tyranny* is probably subjective, but I would have to say that we could look to one magnificent part of our history as a possible time... the beginning of that *road to ruin*.

Conduct

That would be when the sixteenth president, Abraham Lincoln (1809 – 1865) openly, arrogantly, and illegally ignored the United States Constitution and waged his war of aggression against the South.

Lincoln had been spoon-fed Communism by associates of Karl Marx (1818 – 1883) and regularly exchanged letters with Marx. Lincoln's politics, taxing, banking, conscription, corruption, spending, expropriation, gratuities, and overall Conduct to draft, deploy a military force, and wage a devious agenda against "his own" bears this out. He had plenty of support from many so-called "elected officials" and countless others as well. Lincoln had little interest in the slavery issue. His war was almost entirely an economic engagement. Worse, when his inability to sustain that war started to surface, and the Confederates were making progress defending themselves, his advisors would come up with an amazing move that would change the character of wars and politics around the world.

Understanding how important this move would be requires knowing that every nation with an army and navy had a very keen interest in how Lincoln's war was going. His war would influence how other nations would dole out or withhold their support for the North, or South, and be willing or not, to engage in other conflicts under consideration, but not yet started.

Lincoln was a fairly smart person and knew he was running out of money, men and hardware. He started a war he now realized he could not win without the assistance of "outsiders." With the help of many people who may, or may not, have had a "dog in *his* fight," he came up with the solution. Lincoln would step up with the *Emancipation Proclamation* and add a completely new dynamic to the situation. His war suddenly became less an issue of economics and more an issue of *emotion* about *freeing* the slaves. The Proclamation was an imperfect document, but the effect around the globe was huge. Now there were nations willing to "chip in" with the North, causing others to withdraw from the South. In other words, the Proclamation was an enormous and crushing *fund-raiser.*

It would take the involvement of the bankers and others to raise foreign money, men and ships to save their own wealth and win Lincoln's devious war for him, but the impetus of the North-South conflict had little or nothing to do with any slavery. Lincoln was an expert talking head and made enemies in the North *and* South. The wreckage of the North-South war inflicted losses on just about everyone in the form of death, destruction, loss of wealth and misery of all manner.

Mercy! That whole story sounds familiar for today, doesn't it?! Money, power, ego and politics equals misery and wars! Bummer...

Let us all keep some little details in mind. Whatever *you* think about the North-South Conflict, and whether the war served or saved anyone... absolutely does not matter. The winners and liars likely provide most "history" that you might *think* you know. You get *their* version... past and present. I guess you could call it, "The last man standing story." *You* get the survivor's fairytale... maybe. Since we're here, I might add that I have problems with the North-South Conflict referred to as the *Civil War.* The Southern States wanted *out,* and were attacked by Lincoln, to be driven back *in,* with new rules of compliance. Remember, Lincoln also had "handlers." We might see a *real* civil war when America wakes up to reclaim what inside thugs have stolen from them (us). When that day arrives, I hope the reclaiming good guys can *finish the job.*

Conduct

Only real deep digging might give you some truth, and we all know that real *truth* is something few people have any interest in. Golly, gee... no wonder so many people are mad about ideas of which they are patently ignorant. I guess somebody has to cause shipwrecks in calm seas.

Influential people of business, science, history, industry, politics and more, fabricate and/or defend fake stories all the time. Think EPA (Environmental Protection Agency), BLM (Bureau of Land Management), DOE (Dept. of Ed.), Federal Reserve, alphabet agencies and offices of all manner, corporate big wigs and on and on. I suppose we could say, "You are stupid by desire," since we are conditioned to accept their dribble. They are shrinking your head... dude.

> *People will generally accept facts as truth only it the facts agree with what they already believe.*
>
> > \- Andy Rooney (1919 – 2011)

And this –

> *Now, I know among the politically correct, you're not supposed to use facts that are uncomfortable.*
>
> > \- Newt Gingrich (1943 -

So – back to Religion. It now clearly appears that Lincoln was a hard-boiled, cold-blooded communist. That said, I can now declare that he had *no* religion – at least, certainly no *Christian* Religion. The wonderful light of the United States Constitution was *gleefully trashed*, and pretty-much *has been ever since*. Many say that Lincoln's demise was way too late. Moot point now, huh?

By the way – since so many people are stupid in this day and age, maybe I ought to ask, "Do you know what a Communist is?" "Do you even care?" Well, here is my brief definition: *A Communist is any person or group of people, who want you obedient to, and controlled by, them... through any means necessary, including mass murder.* Are you starting to get any smarter? Think China and *Mao.* Then think Pol Pot, Stalin, Amin and plenty more. Fascism too – think Hitler and others.

Okay, so what is a Socialist? A dangerous dirty rat that does the heavy lifting for a Communist.

We are a Capitalist Nation, in case you conveniently forgot. I suppose that at this time in history, you may not have ever been taught capitalism and the benefits therein.

Unfortunately, some of the "history" being shoveled down the throats of our public school children is myth and outright fabricated lies. As far as I am concerned, most monuments of politicians belong under an outhouse. Seems like the least deserving get too much attention. The under-handed, double-dealing that has gone on, and is going on in Washington DC is beyond any understanding when a body tries to describe the magnitude of the crime and corruption. Money and power Conduct, huh?

We need plenty of grand monuments of our great pastors, scientists and pioneers with as much visibility as the political memorials.

Anyway, as religions go, Christianity and Judaism are good ones. You need the whole Bible to get the full meaning, and *getting* that full meaning is easy. From early on, the Biblical Scriptures have guided personal Conduct and laws of the world and this nation.

Conduct

Of course, we know there are a few nations that want nothing to do with anything Biblical. Their Conduct proves it, as well.

It hurts to see Biblical Scripture intentionally misread, misinterpreted or selectively omitted, and then be used to give special-interest people or groups sway and cover over our original Constitutional law. Keep in mind – *a government benefit to one person, is a penalty on another...*

The Bible gives us an excellent look into the past and future and is a "guidebook" on how to Conduct our lives. A whole lot of people do not want to be held to any standards of Conduct, which includes keeping their pants zipped, staying sober, refraining from name-calling, and more.

Looks like part of the problem is with people confusing truthful historical facts with fiction and half-truths that someone else has written or said, or that which ends up in some movie. Therefore, we are back to an old problem that will not go away – the lack of proper education. It is very confusing to me when people I love and respect seem to have an odd take on certain Biblical topics. I know very well that I could be wrong, and *I am still learning,* so I usually swallow hard, keep my trap shut and move on... for the most part.

All right, let us look at a couple of definitions –

Jew – (Biblical, II Kings 16:6, etc.) Name used to designate the kingdom of Judah. A person descended from the Semitic people led by Moses.

Christian – (Biblical, Acts 11:26) A person who believes in Christ and follows his teachings.

Christianity – The whole of the Religion of Christ; founded on the teachings of Jesus Christ.

These definitions were lifted from several dictionary sources, all of which basically said the same thing.

Now then, Jesus the Christ was a Jew whose followers became Christians. So - if we call ourselves, or anyone, a Christian... by extension we have some obvious guidelines within which to Conduct ourselves – right? Jew, Jesus, Judeo-Christian – are you with me here?

Okay – back to the Founding Fathers and this Christian Nation. When the Constitution was written, provisions were made for the immigration of people who were *not* Christians. There were *no* provisions made for *changing* the founding Christian beliefs. That said, we now know that other "religions" could come and enjoy our surroundings, but were bound by *our* Judeo-Christian-based rules of Conduct. For the most part, everything was fairly tame until the muslims showed up with death, destruction and misery. Then they gain political favor. Certainly not mine. Worse, stupid Americans (?) elected a muslim for the country's highest office. Even more worse, the guy was re-elected. See anything here, yet? I find few who will admit they voted for the guy. I suppose it all means the ballots were corrupted and/or people now realizing our peril are liars. Wonderful conduct all the way around, huh?

Therefore – if you decide to "look the other way" defending muslims and their behavior, you can be considered a facilitating Conspirator giving them cover for their deeds. Overtly or covertly ignoring their motives, plans and devastation can now mean you are *willfully endangering others and me.*

Conduct

With a well-documented history of murder by the thousands, mutilation of thousands more, wreckage and damage into the multiple billions of dollars, infestation of our cities, destruction of our culture, intentional and destructive interference with our political system and those of other countries, daily slaughter around the world, outright threats of annihilation of the State of Israel, Jews, Christians and anyone else who dare challenge them, a Middle East war machine under intense development to continue their destruction, horrendous terrorist attacks against us and the world - I think we can say islam is a bone fide and dangerous threat to deal with. All this within the last few decades or so.

If you "feel" like you have to give them sway, I can only assume that you are a coward aiding the enemy. They are most definitely out to conquer the world by any means, and this is not their first run at it. They might be considered a disease that needs a systemic treatment. Research the muslim wars of yesteryear and never forget, "they eat their own."

One of the major dictionaries defined *Christian* as a "presentable person." Give me a break...

Be advised – there is a plethora of people and groups of people purporting to be Christians. Try to get in with the "right" folks. Maybe someone you know who attends a full-gospel church would be a place to start. You have some good choices in the Jewish Realm as well. I'm sure you will find what works for you... or not.

It is easy to say, "If it is good for me, it is good for you." We know better than that. We also know, for instance, that the Catholics have a penchant for control and global conquest, considering that all their Popes have been on board with the United Nations since the inception of that body. Too bad they are so eager to hand over their people and money to a bunch of one-world thugs. Are you sure those Catholics are *Christians*?? Guilty by association, huh? There is a back-story to everything, and religion is no different. Cults, occults, groups, gangs and so on. At least scout around for some ground to find a little peace.

Forgiveness and SALVATION come with Jesus and Christianity. It is free. The Movement of the Lord will give you peace and freedom from worries and concerns. I pray you may experience it for yourself.

Christians and Jews are good people... or, at least, they are supposed to be.

Real charity comes from our heart and labor, not some agenda-driven politician giving away your hard-earned money.

And now, this -

How could I possibly end this particular segment without answering that question screaming in your head, "Okay... what, exactly, faith or church do YOU go to?" I will tell you folks. I attend, support, and recommend the Full Gospel, Charismatic Pentecostal – sometimes referred to as "The Holy Rollers." You can joke about that moniker, but I will take it as a compliment. Anyway, it is here where you and I can see and experience *real* healing. It is here we receive Biblical Teachings that have not been "picked and chosen" or watered down, to please a few people who do not want the *whole* Truth. I'll look for you there, and you can help *me* learn faster. 'Nuff said?

Chapter 6

SEX

Oh Boy!!! Another spicy, hot-button topic…

This is one of those subjects where everybody seems to know too much or not enough. What might be perfectly normal to one person, is twisted and disgusting to another. Therefore, I guess we can agree that the topic of sex is subjective.

For the record – I do not condone or condemn any Conduct within this topic. I only discuss it.

Now then, how does Sex fit into your pattern of Conduct and your future? With great power and authority, that is how!

At this point, we need to revisit the part about keeping your pants or panties, on… or off, depending on your motives. Aside from the instant pleasure of conquering and cataloging another score, there can be far-reaching consequences for a few minutes (seconds?) of this kind of Conduct.

If two people who are on the "prowl" are anywhere near each other, the results of their meeting are probably predictable. Once the decision to find a partner for the scorecard has cleared your conscience, any further action becomes mechanical. Another willing partner, and almost *any* willing partner will do, closes the loop and typically becomes "game on."

At my age of mid-sixties, studying this phenomenon has the components of both fascination and dread.

When I was growing up, the idea of a man and women being together meant the two of them meeting somehow, dating for a while, establishing compatibility, falling in love, and mating for life. The results of that union brought me friends and relatives in childhood and exposed me to the fun of being young. As I grew older and physically matured, I felt the "attraction" and started wondering on whom to focus my thoughts. Coming from my well-grounded background, I could only dream and hope for what the future might bring. Then, something else happened. The friends and relatives I grew up with were having the same emotions, with a huge difference – many were not held to my standard of that "grounding," or more correctly, Biblical Conduct. Soon enough, the pressure was on to join that cabal and compare notes of our Conduct. To me, the thought of sharing any information about something *that* personal was very bad. Worse, once the private information was out, it fell into the hands of people who wanted to gain favor with others about who is doing whom. I was young and confused, but not stupid. I disassociated myself from that group.

Conduct

My testosterone did not slow down; I just kept my trap shut and moved on. That rounds out the "fascination" part.

The dread part has been with me for many years. I think I recognized it early in life, certainly more so now, and it comes from the Conduct I saw then and see today. It seems as if two young people pair off and get it "on" without a kiss, and immediately go looking for another score. Disease and depression might be close behind. Dangerous Conduct in some circles.

So, how do these youngsters come to this? Easy. They have had years to study their parents and at this date, probably their grandparents and it is monkey-do. Immorality... bummer.

It does not take a degree in science to marvel at the percentage of divorces among the married. That number by itself is staggering, so I guess I can infer that their relationships had a sexual component with little or no emotional or intellectual attraction. Further adding dread are the children that come of these loveless unions. They have to go somewhere... even in the toilet as an abortion.

But, wait a minute! Don't look at me as if I am the morality police! There is plenty of time to enjoy Good Conduct in bed or wherever you choose. It will be orders-of-magnitude better if you genuinely care about your partner, preferably a spouse.

Sometimes, some of the seemingly oddest pairs of people have a very special relationship. They might be steady partners; they might be total strangers, maybe a husband and wife, who knows? They might be cousins, neighbors and people who never see each other – in public. They enjoy a compatibility that seems to transcend friendship. They appear to be in a level of peace, grace and movement that no one can figure out.

Remember, the topic here is sex. I am all in for the strong emotional bonds that build wonderful families, but that is not where this segment of my paper is going. We are heading for the kind of pleasure that is enjoyed by the few who care about *real* sex. Their goal is absolute, mind-bending, memory-making joy of sex. Heights of meaningful sexual experience that are mentally distracting years later. It is the kind of distraction that takes the mind off anything but sex. Years later, it is the kind of distraction that makes a person think they would rather be somewhere else with *someone* else. It is real and it is difficult to understand. The memories eventually cool in intensity, but I doubt they ever go completely away. If the memory-making experience takes place with your spouse, you have it "made" in ways few can understand. If anyone will say much about it, it is usually a reference to the "wild side," not to be confused with a song by the musical group *Motley Crue*. This is wild behavior with subjective Conduct. It teaches you secrecy of the highest order and it is legal, folks… that is all…

Then, of course, there is physical damage in sexually transmitted diseases, emotional wreckage looming and the story can go on and on…

This all is probably the kind of Conduct you should avoid. Having sex is one thing - being a cheap genderless whore is quite another. It can affect the circumstances of your future as an unclean lifestyle. Unclean usually equates to bad up-bringing and little experience in circles of importance. Once the word is out that you are making the "rounds," you become a liability to avoid. People who are a little higher on the information curve know how bad conduct in bed has bad consequences in general and try to be a little more selective of their choices in life and their partners. Debased morality has a price. A great day for condoms, huh?

Don't look to me for graphic details - I am not a tour guide.

Now then, how does all this play into your overall search for success? Well, with all the bad sexual Conduct out there, I can only say that you need *good* sexual Conduct. That might be one of those oxymoron's, but it will have to do...

Be clean, look clean and smell clean. Personal hygiene cannot be over-emphasized. Let the "human pheromones" do the talking. You have no idea who you are going to meet or how they are about to change your life. Stay away from smelly colognes and perfumes – they tend to act as a warning. I cannot recommend any tattoos or exotic piercings either. They tend to suggest a willfulness to act with shady Conduct, creating an exposure issue for a potential partner. Speak properly, stand straight, look ahead, not down, and move with smoothness. This provides the air of importance and dignity. As a predator in the hunt, your prey is anyone who can further your objective (or, agenda). Sometimes there is instant chemistry that sweeps two people straight to an immediate encounter. Could be someone's kitchen counter, a hallway, maybe an airliner's lavatory – it happens. Hollywood movies play on this theme.

There are a high percentage of happy couples who do very well with good old missionary sex. They might try something different, but a happy couple none-the-less. They have a strong bond, are very loyal to each other, and very happy *with each other.*

Then there are the couples who are happily married with a weak sex life. That's dangerous. The happily separated couple who think they are going to "work it out" are probably full of wishful thinking and have created a danger zone as well. Sometimes they regroup, but usually with damage. Couples have no idea how long they will stay happy, but sometimes a secret affair keeps the happiness intact... so we are told. We only know when their relationship starts to fold, and the cheating spouse then throws the news in the face of the former mate.

Of course, there are happily married couples who are too busy for a meaningful sex life. Real danger here. They might as well be walking around with a target pinned on. They'll really be happy then, huh? And, then, there is the happy couple who appear to "have it all," and something is missing. I wonder what? Your "pheromone detection" and diminishing Character will probably find it soon. This might figure to be a time when someone supposedly of good Character gets a pass for being a liar. Mercy... I told you this might get bumpy.

If you open your trap about a tryst, devastation will loom on the horizon. Do not do or say something stupid trying to impress anyone - it is trouble. An allusion to any sexual Conduct in the company of others will promptly be seized upon as admission of questionable Conduct and result in accusations that become impossible to undo. Whatever you *meant* to say does not matter anymore. You can only hope the people in audience will not shun you for a misunderstood piece of information. Look at it from their perspective. Their mind is telling them that any remarks made could have been about them. As I said before, you do not know how others will play into your future. Keep the trap clamped.

Conduct

Then, again – there are those who will listen with both ears to any talk of sex. They might put you in their own crosshairs for a punch on *their* scorecard. Brushing off or playing into sexual advances is best done with some tact. The person making those advances might be in a position to wreck your life and career. By the same token, they could just as easily pave your road with gold to the future. My-oh-my... now what? Depends. Are you willing to scrap the companionship and feelings of an existing partner? Are you willing to say *no* at any price? Do you have any partner? On a factory floor, you might have some immunity. In an office, things change and with fewer employees, the person making the advances best not be a boss or relative in *that* business. Sex in the workplace is tricky. You may never see it, or you might be too stupid to recognize it, but people are watching. It is dangerous ground and requires awareness. Watch your Conduct.

Incidentally, just in the for-what-it-is-worth column, think of all the people in a stage act or entertainment of some sort, who could not resist the lust and lure of a groupie. Holy cow, Elsie!

More than one of them ended up with a family – seemingly out of the clear, blue sky! I guess for a hit-and-run like *that*, predictability of outcome and lineage was not very high on the planning list. The same could be said for those folks *trolling* for a similar encounter, huh? Pant and panty issues, I suppose. A high-priced couple of seconds, eh? More condoms, Mac!

And now, P & P –

Yes, ladies and gentlemen, how could I ever address the topic of Sex without spending at least a couple minutes about the behavior of prostitution and pornography?

Actually, the whole discussion is very short. First, we remember that this is Sex, and it can be normal or twisted, right? The old "subjective" interpretation. Anyway, for purposes of this discussion, we will just refer to the Conduct as "Sex" and go from there.

In the Prostitution arena, we have people exchanging something of value for the engagement. We make no distinction between who is providing the service and who is receiving, nor do we concern ourselves with how many people are involved. We also draw no conclusions or make any allegations about practice, pain or pleasure when the players include the use of mechanical accessories, ropes, chains and implements of all manner. The folks who engage in Sex are presumed to enjoy it. So, we now need not make any distinction between straight and wild side Sex, and eliminated any problems with opposite and same-Sex encounters. I am not making any morality calls here... just discussion.

So far, the only difference between activities of choice and partners, is the exchange of value... probably money, but could be anything.

Moving on, the practice of prostitution is considered by many as a high-risk behavior and therefore has been banned or carefully regulated. Arguably, the biggest risk is sexually transmitted disease, which can cripple and kill. More risk might be about profit and jealousy when the prostitutes are handled by pimps and profiteers and/or try to maintain a relationship outside of the profit motive. Then we have the "sleaze factor" with all the alcohol, drugs, filth and hygiene issues, insects, all the broken hearts, homes, bones, bottles and more, including death and murder. That, folks, pretty-much wraps up the topic of prostitution. Another tidbit I can add is the fact that there can be near-by, high-dollar players who you may never know about. Some of these 'tutes have families and are clean, high-standard whores. Is that an oxymoron??

So, what about pornography? Well, this is really short – take all of that Sex and prostitution behavior, put it in films, videos, magazines, and any other media, then package it for sale to the public, and you have pornography. This is also high-risk behavior – legal, emotional and more.

Okay, I think that should do it. I will skip the entertainment part and move on.

According to additional wisdom from Socrates - *The hottest love has the coldest end.*

CHAPTER 7

WORKPLACE

Once again, experience has taught me that if you are in the company of people who think as you think, the level of potential conflict is somewhat reduced. Being in certain *specific* groups can put the level of conflict-risk near zero and allow the generation of great ideas and excellent productivity. However, I am afraid that for the majority of people, a compromise in the mix of people is as good as it gets. Sometimes those compromises can get brutal. In the arena of the office and factory-floor, politics can make or break a career path or even workplace tolerability. The playing field becomes a dog-eat-dog mentality with winners and losers.

The types of people who play the *office*-politic card are a lowly, despicable group. They know when to take a cheap shot at, or talk down to, a fellow employee in the presence of others to gain a few seconds of notoriety. It is usually at some intellectual or emotional expense to the offended party. This Conduct can be a reference to an earlier and harmless chance mistake, but usually is a derogatory and intentional effort to discredit someone.

Having spent over twenty-five years in various production and manufacturing facilities, I have seen good people who had a lot to offer, become victimized by some jealous person trying to impress others for personal and political gain to enhance their power in the office or authority in the facility. What I find so offensive about these players is the complicity of management giving them a pass on serious infractions of common decency. Being on both sides of the supervisor's desk over the years, I have seen and heard a lot of offensive gestures and remarks. *I* am also experienced at *counter*-offense.

The way to handle this issue is by doling out superior and hateful rebuttals, absolutely guaranteed to hurt feelings and crush egos. I go after them with diminished importance, demonized behavior, highlighted shortcomings, and references to physique, speech and dress. If all that hasn't gotten their attention, I pour-it-on about their family members, sex, friends and pets. This style of conflict resolution gives me an excellent sense of pride and self-worth. Besides, all of the people who are not paralyzed with fear… or ducking… might be laughing.

If you are in a meeting or open office and confronted with this crude political Conduct, I recommend a brief look around to see if anybody is going to condemn the remark. If not, then it becomes an open conflict with the goal of uncompromised victory. A barb or two about their authority to make such a remark will either stop it or intensify it. You might even have a vice-president or some other corporate officer in attendance that will open their trap and say something stupid like, "Okay, okay, that's enough!" WHOA! See what happened here? No condemnation of the behavior of the person who started it. So far, the creep has marched on to your turf, fired a demeaning salvo, and been given a blessed pass.

Now your status is further diminished as the brunt of the derogatory remark *and* censoring. It becomes decision time, folks. In just a couple of seconds, you have been diminished, leashed, muzzled and caged... maybe.

I can tell you, again from personal experience, that your job and any prestige that went with it, will now deteriorate and continue to do so as long as you remain in their employ. At this point, you are naked and marked. I strongly recommend open boardroom warfare because now you have at least two buttheads holding you in the bowl and itching to flush. It is time to mow the dirt flat.

This is the point of no return and your big guns must come out. If you are a namby-pamby, then tear up, shut up and sit down - or leave. If you are a leader, point fingers at them and do a tirade of accusations and demonizing. Get into their psyche. You now have the upper hand with shock factor on your side. A line that worked for me over the years is, "Just because your whoring biological parents hated you, doesn't mean *I* deserve your despicable resentment." Does this sound a little harsh? I can only say that you will probably be smiling soon. They might apologize and restore the meeting... or fire you. It absolutely does not matter. If you are forced to cash in chips, get your moneys' worth. These things go fast. From start to finish is only about ten to fifteen seconds. Tell yourself, "I'm ready for my Good Conduct Ribbon."

So now, I suppose the question becomes, "why not show under-standing and compassion and counsel those children of God?" The short answer is, "turf war victory and gratification." There is a time and place for the saintly approach.

Our immoral society has ruined just about everything that used to be important, respectful and appreciated. In today's workplace, being a nice guy seems to diminish authority. Soon enough, either the union, management or both will want to chat. It is not right, and I know it is a horrible thing to say, but... "Nice guys seem to come in last." Somewhere there is a point between being a testy, stiff-necked robot strutting around with a rulebook, and that of being a tolerable, pleasant and firm fellow walking around with the same rulebook. Deal with it... the right way.

On two occasions, I have faced a toe-to-toe standoff that could have gone terribly bad. The first time was a situation where the employee got in my face and told me to *shove it!* I simply got right back in his face and sternly stated that there were three possibili-ties now in his life – do the job; quit and leave; or face my brand of workplace violence. With eyes like saucers, the employee went back to work and later became a good performer.

I have no use for stupid workplace laws or rules that make anything more complicated than what is going down now – this very instant. The clowns making the rules and writing those laws have never punched a time card or supervised real people in a real workplace. Like I say, "broken laws, broken bones or corpses... the deed is done and the authorities will be right along to file a report."

Conduct

The second confrontation was a tad more risky. I was a midnight supervisor in a very hard and dirty facility where turnover was high. A couple of the workers, who had been there for a few years, were good at what they did. I came on duty to broken production machines that had been down all day. I insisted that the lead mechanic give me another eight hours to get the machines going. He told me he had been there all day, half the night and was going home. I repeated myself about another shift. He grabbed a wrench, put his nose right up to my nose, and started to huff and puff. Realizing I was in way too deep, I looked into his eyes and apologized. He felt committed to finish what he had started and began breathing harder. Again, I apologized, only this time it was out of stark fear. I did not unlock my eye contact, but he read my mind and backed off. As he was leaving, I continued to apologize and verbally condemn myself for treating him badly. He simply said he was leaving and left. He came back all right… the next day to get his tools and quit. I tried desperately to keep him on, but I had pee'd in my own coffee and I knew it. I lost the best man on staff. Although the plant continued to run, it was going badly since the machines were old, worn out and needing constant crisis repairs. I lasted another month or so and also quit. The plant closed a few months later. I imagine the positive aspect in this story can be found in a funeral home some time later, after one of our old mutual working cohorts died. We crossed paths at the viewing and it was a grand reunion of cheer and apology with both of us almost weeping. More of that good Conduct and Character-building, I reckon.

CHAPTER 8

DRINK

There may be times when a strong drink sounds good, or a lover, or perhaps some quality time in faith. Since I brought it up, let's talk about that *drink*.

The smell of alcohol is unmistakable and can kill a lot of personal interfacing. If you spent the night twisting tops, the "morning after" smell can have profoundly worse side-affects.

Trying to place some sort of a dollar number on the damage caused by alcohol consumption to people, places, machines, careers, achievements, bank accounts, real estate and any other kind of asset or plan, probably cannot be calculated. I do not doubt there is a demographic study detailing how much who drinks, but - the hidden and obvious costs are staggering.

I remember well as talk-show host G. Gordon Liddy tried to impress upon his listeners the destructive consequences of alcohol. Years later, I remembered and acted on that advice.

Folks, I am telling *you*, alcohol is a friend you do not want. I know perfectly well that many people can have a glass or two of wine, a highball, or a good cold beer occasionally. However, if drinking becomes a habit of every night, it can lead to hard bottles every week. It is easy to do. Alcohol has a strange allure – always there, predictable results and no arguments. Control yourself.

I imagine mind-bending drugs have a similar effect, but without the alcoholic side-affects. Does not matter – your clear-thinking and physical abilities are compromised, or worse. Drug and alcohol impairment can ruin everything that is important to you, and others. The record books are full of the misery caused by this impairment in the form of family, financial and employment loss, murders and maiming with all sorts of implements, and eventually the loss of friends and relatives who tried to help.

In studies of alcohol and drug problems, we will find the police ledgers chocked full of cases where alcohol and drug-crazed people have committed heinous acts. Excessive Alcohol and Drugs will affect many people in ways that their Conduct will be nothing like their normal actions. This is complicated, but I will try to hit a point or two we recognize and leave it at that.

One of the most visible alcohol problems is with drunk drivers. When they cause a problem, it is quite often of magnificent proportions, garnering a great deal of news coverage. It should. The carnage, hurt and grief that goes with loss of limb, life or mobility is permanent.

Conduct

Physical damage messes up your life. Suppose you were experiencing some personal difficulties. The damage of a drunks' wreck can push you over the edge if the driver tears up your body and property. Insurance? We hope. What about crashing into another drunk who was almost home? You may know a family that has been affected in this manner. But, as I said, the drunk driver just happens to be the most visible - it can get worse. An awful lot of drinkers are not particularly stable in the first place. They often have a short emotional fuse and the alcohol can trigger an urge to cry in a beer joint or a violent impulse to do something terribly wrong. Violence associated with alcohol has filled volumes of records. Those records contain the evidence of the particular kind of violence, and it is not for the squeamish. The carnage caused by a deranged, violent drunk is legendary. Screaming, stabbing, beating, slashing, gouging, hanging, shootings – and more.

Okay, what about a non-violent drunk who is not behind the wheel? I'd say this is where a lot of alcohol damage occurs and never makes any news outside of the home, workplace, church or ward. Some folks will get married as drinkers because the drinking had a hand in their meeting in the first place. Depending on their emotional stability, that arrangement may work out just fine. It can all go down badly when the woman gets pregnant and eventually ends up carrying a damaged fetus. It *is not* good folks. In addition, as their drinking increases and the emotions intensify, the blame game sets in and the swinging starts. Makes no difference who started it – just, game on. Nearly the same in beer joint fights. Bummer.

Drunken gamblers are dangerous. Their mind has been softened and they place bets no sane person would touch. I'm talking about casinos, commodities, stocks, options and more. A drunk at the computer keyboard can flatten a family fortune in short order. And speaking of keyboards – drunks will send emails-from-hell to people they actually care about, and completely forget about it. Same thing with phone calls. They will place and receive calls, say stupid things nobody can understand, and have little or no recollection of anything. Not good.

The wreckage caused by a sober parent who becomes a drunk is horrible as well. The side affects can take a happy family to hell through a number of ways, but there is a different dynamic when children are involved. Now you have bosses, neighbors, teachers, police, friends and all the social services dissecting and controlling your life. With or without kids, entertaining work associates who can grease the rails of your advancement is out. Those same people are now trying to figure out how to get rid of you. Some people come through it sobered up and okay.

Stay away from alcohol. The softened brain brings damage, jail, insurance problems, embarrassment, and ruined lives at too high a price. What else can I say? This is one of those low spots where your Conduct will flaw your Character. It takes years to heal.

CHAPTER 9

DRUGS

I suppose as drug use goes, one of the most well-known cases is that of Charles Manson, who, with some of his followers, went on a murder and mayhem binge. A lot of carnage, hurt and grief here. Drugs cause people to do these things. An emotionally weak person, and especially a person with a predisposition to anti-establishment thinking, is a powder keg with a burning fuse when on drugs. It has not been too long ago that stories were in the news of potheads, drug addicts, human zombies on mind-benders, and the weak-minded people following them around who were in communes hanging together sharing pot, pills, needles, sex and who knows what else? Their minds were essentially burned out and concerned family members had to hire special people to physically corral their loved ones and bring them back to their home and reality. It did not always work out well. Numerous addicts preferred the drug-induced euphoria and the filth that went with it, to being in the clean surroundings of friends and loved ones. It is still going on with less attention. I cannot remember how many people I know who have placed their loved ones in rehab units time after time and finally had to give up. Those concerned parents and loved-ones lost big time – money, cars, homes and part of their own sanity – trying to save a son, daughter, brother, sister, and others from the ravages of drugs.

If you look up my distant past, you will find a drug bust with my name featured on the front page of the local paper. There were NO drugs. The editor got his jollies over a bogus bust. Messy and expensive. I was supposed to go to staging battalion for Viet Nam the next day.

Then there are the circumstances of an encounter with a drug addict who needs a fix, or a derelict who wants notoriety. It can be any mugger with no interest in the sanctity of life who wants your money and valuables.

Now what are you going to do? Are you going to fetch your phone and call 9-1-1? Trust me on this one – your ass just might be going under the grass. I'll cover that topic shortly.

CHAPTER 10

CATEGORIES

Conduct of your life will most likely fall into three categories – deliberate, responsive and instinctive. Impressing upon you the importance of deliberate *education* is comparable to a volcano eruption. I cannot say enough about this topic. Some people have a knack for picking up ideas from others and remembering them forever. Most of us, however, need instruction and guidance to get the information we need for the proper Conduct in our lives.

The old phrase "experience is the best teacher" has a lot to do with our development as we mature and move through life. When we are little kids, and mommy is cooking, creating good smells, interesting sights and a hot stovetop, we have a desire to explore the situation. So our curiosity to learn takes us to the scene where we deliberately touch a hot pan, responsively recoil from the instant pain, and instinctively run to mommy looking for comfort. We have just developed some experience and now learn *that* Conduct can hurt twice. Once for the initial Conduct and maybe again for ignoring mommy's commands to get back. Many good people come from good parents who administered a spanking from time-to-time, or required some sort of punishment for bad Conduct and stood by that requirement. Then, again, some people never learn – psychos, criminals, delinquents, idiots and villains of all manner are everywhere. Try to tell the guy who has been doing "it" wrong for thirty years how to do "it" *right*… then tell *me* what you found out.

Experience is another Conduct that can go the good and bad ways. I hope you don't have to give up too much to find out. Many folks will learn how to be smart and pleasant, deliberately parlaying those qualities into a productive future for the benefit of us all. For another class of people, experience will teach them how to profit from inflicting loss, hurt and misery on others. Bad people deliberately do bad things. Worse, usually their profit requirements are very small, but cause enormous damage and suffering on others, forcing a response that ranges from sorrow to revenge.

Education and training create memory. Memory creates the ability to design and react. Repetition creates the ability to react instinctively. So, whether you are flying an airplane through the mountains in a snowstorm, or facing a life or death threat, your instinct can carry you without studying a methodology to deal with your crisis. Instinct works other ways also. After all, where did *you* come from?

Some actions can be a hard lesson with instant or delayed consequences. I wish I could have remembered my education about the

Conduct

destructive side-affects of vocalizing *sarcasm* and *ridicule*. Those devils have cost me the friendship of people who are important to me. There are still folks "out there" who I know to have offended, and I don't know how to make it "right." It is not much fun carrying around the guilt. I have spent hours writing letters, making phone calls and doing internet searches trying to find people deserving an apology from me. I have made contact with folks who appreciated my efforts and have restored our friendship. There are, however, a couple of folks left who I think deserve some sort of acknowledgement, but I have not the guts to re-enter their lives and stir up old emotions. I wonder if this experience falls into the *responsive* Conduct category? For a long time, I was a cocky know-it-all, pickled in alcohol. Maybe it is all resultant Conduct ...?? Bad Conduct by any measure, Bud.

Deliberate Conduct with bad consequences can be forced upon you by others with little or nothing you can do about it. Your response to these forces is predictable by the perpetrators, and your instinct to deal with them can go badly. If you guessed *politics and agenda's*, take a bow. Actions, consequences, experience, history, and hope are all a weak match for power and greed.

> *Good judgment comes from experience, and a lot of that comes from bad judgment.*
>
> - Will Rogers (1879 – 1935)

CHAPTER 11

FIREARMS
(GUNS)

Let's visit the Second Amendment...

Firearms are tools. Tools can and will be misused. Severely regulating tools, or banning tools, has consequences. When the numbers are crunched... all the carnage caused by medical incidents, vehicle crashes, domestic violence, workplace violence, hangings, muggings, murders, rapes, robberies and so on, which included *no* firearms, added to the number of mean, predatory criminals who *do* use firearms... it makes *any* reference to the dangers of *lawful firearm ownership* an unequivocally irresponsible and reckless condemnation of a *non-issue*.

Self-defense is so important you absolutely must have rapid access to a firearm. It is important, of course, to have a solid knowledge of how to use it. When a criminal is breaking down your front door, what is the first thing you do? You dial 9-1-1 to call a man with a gun. What if you are asleep and the criminal is breaking down your bedroom door? Are you still going to take the time to make that call? Of course you will try... maybe. Even if you are fast enough to push those buttons on your phone, remember this - *when seconds count, the cops are only minutes away.* The knowledge and use of a firearm can change the whole dynamic. If you have no stomach for your own defense, you may well be another statistic with your name in another official report. If you survive your attack, you will spend the rest of your life thinking and wondering about it.

All that said, I implore upon you to get facts from reliable sources and **not** campaign to deny someone else the right to their own defense. The government is not a reliable source of information about anything, and particularly any reference to self-defense and firearm statistics. Trying to get meaningful information from the internet on special topics like guns and crime is becoming more difficult as the government pressures various search engines to scrub sites. A lot of internet search-engine operators and owners are also on board with the government in restricting and censoring information. Going to any alphabet agency site reveals little or no information or, worse, intentional bad information. Given the speed with which the politicos are destroying this country by oppressive laws, taxes, soft terror treatment and other crime, you will probably need self-defense from the very people who are supposed to protect you. Think I'm kidding? Take a good, long look at various court rulings to see who is making illegal law, and then take another good look at who is in jail, and who ought to *be* in jail. If you spend any time at all thinking the SCOTUS (Supreme Court of the United States) is on your side, think again. Those appointed criminals have all but scrapped the Bill of Rights and the Constitution of the United States.

Let's remember New Orleans' Katrina, and the wholesale illegal disarming of perfectly good people. How about Canada and the Mounties breaking in, raiding the homes of flood victims and stealing their firearms? Have you ever heard of Tyranny? What do you think our Constitutional framers had in mind with that Second Amendment? Remember this – Armed people are *Citizens*; disarmed people are *subjects*. Our proper Conduct in these affairs is paramount.

"Gun Proofing" children and adults can be accomplished at all ages. Simply put, this is the teaching of firearm safety and proper, effective use. I hope many people get involved and work on safety, accuracy and speed.

Carrying a gun has massive implications. Be sure you know what the risks and expectations are. Keep a clear head - you might actually need it!

Of course, if you are an America-hating liberal who enjoys and takes pleasure in stripping away personal rights and freedoms, then my advice will likely be met with hate and contempt. It also makes you complicit and guilty of facilitating the criminal actions of others who wish to do *me* harm. Now it all makes a body ponder pre-emptive strikes just to stay alive, doesn't it?! So much for "live and let live." Who says, "Crime doesn't pay?" More liars, I reckon.

Now this - The definition of the word "terrorist" has been morphed into whatever some liberal (democrat, communist, etc.) thinks it ought to be. Suffice it to say, "If a person or a group of people are coming to do you *harm*, they are terrorists." That said, it looks as if we can lump politicians right in there also, doesn't it? It is just that political crooks send their armies and henchmen to do the deeds, with your money, of course. You still need your defensive tools and the will to use them. *Your **will** had better be stronger than any fear you might have.* Hmmm, I wonder why?

Before we go to the next topic, let's talk about the *other* Nine Amendments for a minute.

Seems like a lot of folks think those Amendments have strength-in-meaning by their placement in the Bill of Rights. Not hardly... the First or Third, or Tenth – are all on equal footing in importance. That is why they are collectively called the Bill of Rights. You can be sure the other Nine Amendments are under political attack no less than the Second. I suppose you could call the Second Amendment the protector of the other Nine – since it is a high-visibility "lightning rod" for political demonization. Unfortunately, the other Amendments, and particularly the First, have already been targeted and/or stripped or gutted, to muzzle opposition to the destruction of virtually everything else. *Everything* folks – from the printed page to your physical ability to function outside the constraints and dictates of some vague political edict open to corrupt interpretation.

The First Amendment – Let us zero in on this, as well.

Conduct

When someone allows me to know he or she is a "journalist," my BS Alarm goes into overdrive. I have to ask, "Oh really? What *kind* of journalist?" An awful lot of so-called "journalists" probably comprise the largest accumulation of dumpster-scum anywhere. Most people who write for the mass media and most people who get in front of a national news camera as a "reporter" are positively disgusting. They withhold important information and hand out agenda-driven misinformation with impunity. Of course, there are numerous cases where the "reported" news is wrong because the writer/reporter is stupid. It does not matter. This cowardly group of people is so big, and has maligned the First Amendment with such hysteria, mounting a challenge to the corruption and cover-up is very difficult. Freedom of Speech is one thing... using that freedom for the intentional destruction of any other Freedom is criminal Conduct. Prosecution, anyone? I wonder if any of those liars even have a conscience? Lying and prevailing Conduct, folks...

Well... not a civics class here, but are you getting an idea of where your Bill of Rights has gone?

Let me cheerfully move on and talk about muggers...

CHAPTER 12

MUGGERS

Mugging situations on the street, in the mall, the theater, grocery store parking lot, post office, summer camp, church, school
or anywhere, can all be lumped together and called *encounters of
the worst kind.* Being mugged is a frightful, shocking, life-altering
event... if you survive it. The experience could just as easily be
a life-*ending* event. There is a growing disregard for human life
as our irresponsible government continues to meddle in personal
and public affairs, *limiting* and *reversing* progress with respect to
our advancement and safety as a human populous.

My assessment of the situation is simple – it starts in Washington,
DC. The politicos have diminished the value of human existence
in the U.S. of A. by debasing human behavior through a myriad of
complex laws that favor special-interest groups and scraps morality.
I take no issue with those certain groups of people, but I take serious

offense at having the government-sponsored special interest agendas rubbed in my face day in and day out, with the associated high price tag. We are persecuted and prosecuted for normal, responsible, productive daily Conduct. Think "thought police."

Having so much government emphasis on all kinds of "wars" does not bode well either. The word "war" is supposed to describe some sort of conflict involving shooting and killing on a battlefield. Now the politicians give us wars on drugs, women, terror, poverty and who knows what else. Just as bad, the presidential cabinet is made up of "czars," a term usually associated with Russian emperors. See where this is going? How about the official war on YOU? Surely, you do not believe all those federal laws are going to thwart some terrorist, drug deal or mugger. I'll bet a lot of people think the crippling price tag for being a producing U.S. Citizen funds the *tooth fairy*.

You might have a brilliant career finding out where the *real* drug traffic is, and *who* is running the show. Maybe do some investigative Conduct for amusement and shock factor… if you survive.

Well now - we have street *and* political *czars* waging *war* on easily toppled territory – you and me. What are you going to do? Maybe you could tell your favorite politician to outlaw muggings. Or, maybe you can wake up and realize that politicians are an arrogant bunch of liars who have no interest in your safety. As a matter-of-fact, they are *very* interested in *stripping* you of any means to deal with any kind of threat. Keep in mind the court has ruled the police have *no duty to protect the general public* [Warren v. District of Columbia (444 A.2d. 1, D.C. Ct. of Ap. 1981)]. *YOU have a clear-cut obligation to protect yourself and your loved ones.* Your absolute best means to this end is through the ownership of, and skill to use, a firearm. Muggings and personal attacks go down fast. From the time you realize that you are in imminent danger, until the time it is over, is somewhere in the vicinity of about two to ten seconds or so. An assailant with a knife can be far more dangerous than one with a gun since it is quiet, concealable and easily available. If you see a mugger on the street, and he has a knife, I hope you have your affairs in order. That mugger can close a twenty-five-foot distance in about one and a half seconds, and when he arrives, it will not go well. Most of everything you hear and see in any "news" about guns is myth or out-right fabricated lies. Street thugs won't be buying any guns at the store. Thugs will acquire their hardware through another heinous murder, mugging, burglary, or robbery somewhere else. More carnage, of course... just routine criminal Conduct.

What's a body to do? Two things – be aware and prepare.

First - Always be aware of your surroundings, avoiding scary areas and proximity to suspicious people. Maintain some sort of order in your life and use a levelheaded approach to a dangerous situation.

Second - Learn something. Talk to others about this. Take a self-defense course or personal survival course. Get yourself a reliable firearm and train with it. After you train with it, keep it close... *real* close... and then continue the training.

As to that bedside attack, have your ducks in a row. Know where your defensive tools are, have the training and the will to use them, and then counter-attack knowing that failure is out-of-the-question. Never, ever, *lay there and hope to live through it.* You kill first, because the perp (perpetrator) has massive damage in mind for you. Heavy sleepers might want a door alarm.

There is another criminal ploy in play that is gaining in popularity and occurrences. It is sometimes called "take-over assault" where the bad guys show up in groups of two or more to annihilate their prey, have their way, then rob and destroy at will. Makes that six-round magazine limit look swell, doesn't it?

I may be a little "windy" with all of this, but as you now know, I really care! I care about you, I care about myself, and I care about our country... at least, what is left of it.

Now then – suppose you have just completed your third and final interview for the job of your dreams and it is time for some refreshment. You are elated at the prospects because the only hurdle left is the negotiation of that top-dollar salary. So you stop in at the nearest convenience store for refreshments, pick out pop and candy and are standing in line for the cashier. Without any warning, a perp blows through the door, gun drawn and orders everybody down. Now what? Well, forget anything you have seen in movies and been told by know-it-alls. You have no idea what this perp plans to do, but you do know it is not going to be good. The perp could be drunk or on drugs... but, so what? My recommendation is keeping that level head, glancing around at the situation, and figure out a way to RUN... or *attack* the perp. You attack to kill! Now *split seconds* count and if you are *able - draw, aim* and *shoot*! If not, then grab bottles, cans or anything to throw... scream, distract and attack! Gouge, scratch, stab, bite, kick and rip... *if* you can. Rule number one for any impending fight – avoid and RUN!

Conduct

Rule number two – engage and WIN! If a cop is standing in line with you, you *might* have a better than zero chance. Otherwise, there will be no time for any cop and you will have little, if any, time to call one. Split seconds count – remember? Don't look for any approval or help from anyone. Your needs at this point are not only clear and urgent, chances are that other people are clueless cowards impeding self-preservation!

I know I will catch some opposition on this next idea because *some* self-defense instructors teach that you cannot draw a weapon on a person who has already drawn on you. Suicide? Homicide? Not me! That despicable and destructive criminal is not there passing out flowers. I have one chance to bob, duck, draw and shoot. I'll take it!

Of course, I suppose you could peacefully file into the beer cooler and take a bullet in the back of your head. C'mon people... wake the hell up!

This might be a good place to compare a variation of True Facts against Fake Facts.

> True Facts – "Another horrible incident by heinous people who have intentionally, blatantly and despicably executed three people and brutally maimed another. The bloody corpses and lone survivor were found in a walk-in cooler. The motive can only be greed, mayhem and robbery."

> Fake Facts – "In tonight's news, another incident of violence at Bessie's market involving more guns again. It looks like another dispute over money and drugs."

I cannot overstate the importance of having that firearm. Just the mere sight of a gun stops thousands of would-be attacks every year. Your Conduct in this arena will give you plenty to talk about ... or *be talked* about. Generally, gunshot survival in the U.S. of A. is somewhere around 80%.

I am very well aware that guns are not for everyone. I also know that many gun owners and non-owners have no interest in personal defense. I further know that many people who have a gun could not use it in a criminal showdown anyway. Use of a gun with inadequate or no training and/or missing your intended target *in* a showdown - might get you maimed, dead or scheduled for training in a prison shower.

HOWEVER – there is hope in people who have the training, stability and fortitude to make the right decisions and do the right actions when the chips are down. Support and encourage this important group of men and women. THAT folks, is Good Conduct.

By the way - exactly what are you going to do when the main economic collapse arrives? *It will arrive...* complete with the roving bands of greedy, starving, horny thugs targeting YOU! I guess you had better have those high-capacity magazines charged up and a plan for *that* Conduct.

Chapter 13

AGE

Getting older has certain benefits. Age gives you a past. Your past gives you experience. Your experience gives you knowledge and a foundation to draw upon for the present and future.

If your past has been a ho-hum life with no real meaning, you probably have little intellect to pass on to offspring or discuss with someone else. If you are a low performer with no real accomplishments to reflect upon, no goal of any matter, and have plenty of friends to share all this with, there is an excellent chance that you are stupid. You might be fat, dirty and stink too.

This type of Conduct is good news to the politicians of late since they can deem you impaired, label you disabled and give you someone else's money. An awful lot of fat, skinny, stupid and smelly people are already labeled and are enjoying all the government handout freebies. Being stupid means you have most of the entire population for company. You get to be labeled as a learning-disabled, mentally challenged kind-of-person. Do you see where this is going? I'll bet a lot of people would argue that I am an arrogant s-o-b. Well, maybe... The big problem here is simple – stupid, dirty and smelly people do not give a flying crap about me. Worse, they give an even lesser crap about themselves. Why shouldn't they? There are legions of people, unions and special interest groups constantly pestering the media, politicians and people in general to give their "cause" a forum and some sort of law for special favor... and... you guessed it - our money. Stupid people are dangerous to you and me, and a gold mine for politicians. Stupid people are easily manipulated into doing, saying or believing whatever dribble their buddy's or handlers can dream up. They have no interest in getting any *true* facts about any issue, have no interest in what you need, want or care about, and definitely have no interest in where the chances of life take *them*. Sounds a little like *indifference*, huh? They are particularly bad about championing causes and people about which they have absolutely no idea and could care less. Hmmm... starting to sound like liberals are in their camp, huh? You can bet your life on that one. Anything to destroy the Constitution. Any tactic to destroy the existing success of free and private enterprise with no plan to replace or improve it. I wonder if it is called Mob Rule?

Mob Rule is a politicians dream. It gives them an issue to stump and promote their agenda of converting our wonderful Republic into a democracy – technically mob rule – where agreement on some vague or personal issue is promoted by numbers of people and wins by sheer force. So much for the rules that are supposed to apply to everybody through the Constitution. Worse, all the crappy unconstitutional laws of now and recent past are being selectively applied. Just peachy...

[*Generalizing in any subject area is always dangerous, so allow me to give myself some cover and clearly state that* I am not without feelings and understanding. *I realize there are people who have unwanted issues they would gladly discard. There are plenty of smart, pleasant, overweight, skinny and handicapped folks who are important people of grace and performance in many areas of life, business and industry. They offer care, labor and love to ALL of us, and have our best interest at heart giving us all an example for which to aspire. IN OTHER WORDS, not everyone is as he or she may appear to you or me. Get the true facts about anything or anyone before casting any aspersions. "Don't judge a book by its cover."* Fair enough?]

In some talk-show circles, this group is kindly referred to as the "low-information group." Did you catch my earlier reference to "true facts"? I imagine most of you did, and probably wondered what that was all about. Well, sadly to say, there are two sets of facts floating around. The first set of facts, the True Facts, has science and evidence to prove something. The second set of facts, the Fake facts, are those pieces of information someone else wants you to believe. It probably has something to do with bringing the phrase *politically correct* and *agendas* to the front and center. Hiding behind political correctness allows devious people to be smiling-face liars. It is cover for most politicians and other communists in our lives to tell the public, or anybody, outright lies, and for the most part get away with it. That Conduct puts the onus of truth on the listener. It forces the listener to accept the lies or challenge the liar. Now the liar can sit back, take pot shots at any challenge, and demonize everything presented. Like I said, "Of all the Character flaws an individual can have, being a liar probably ranks as one of the worst." I am not short-selling murder, but liars tell lies and usually have a buddy or members of the U.S. political system to lie with them, giving all involved false credibility.

On the grand scale of U.S. politics, the liars have a complicit news media giving massive cover by not reporting important develop-ments and changes in the political arena, or fabricating their own story, which may, or may not include the correct, or all, of the information. Challenging a person's view or declaration that is met with any contempt or evasion is a huge red flag. This business of being politically correct has morphed into making a *true* refer-ence to some specific Conduct or topic a near-crime. Maybe not even "near." Wonderful, huh?

A good joke with all the qualities necessary to be truly funny, refer-ring to any person or group of people, can get your *arse* in a serious jam. I mean, after all, it is the absurdity of it that makes anything funny. This arena is ripe for all kinds of Conduct. If you follow me around, you are going find that I am old enough to call fat & stupid exactly what it is. I am sick and tired of ducking because America-hating liberals want to lie and make some sort of politi-cal hay by demonizing me. So there! ...See? Note how I matured with Age.

If you are gathering government paychecks for being lazy and/or stupid, you are not a *Good Guy*. I will pray for you.

Now you know... there is more to Age than bulging belly's, bald heads and wrinkles.

Conduct

Phew, man… that is a lot of interesting material under the heading of *Age*, huh?

Some day you will be old enough to start reading fairy tales again.
- C. S. Lewis (1898 – 1963)

Old age ain't no place for sissies.
- Bette Davis (1908 – 1989)

CHAPTER 14

CLEANING UP

I am getting better at keeping my thoughts to myself. After all, I have only *alienated* most of my family, friends and neighbors by trying to be helpful. In the same vein, I am getting better at emphasizing points with words that are not so blue and graphic. I am also cleaning up my roadside manner by sparing lousy drivers my version of the "highway bird." You would be impressed by how many friends I have called to apologize for *that* bad Conduct. I also have a polished cover story for offending my friends who cannot drive right. I suppose I am a Christian *work-in-progress* who is cleaning up Conduct and building Character. *I love and forgive you all*, and I pray *you* are strong enough to see past my shortcomings and forgive *me*.

An awful lot of people will make passionate speeches and declarations using the Bible as their reference. I would have to say that few, if any, have read the whole book. They are people I refer to as *part-time* or *non*-Christians, distorting Biblical passages they have picked and chosen to further some agenda. In addition, I will say this – you cannot be a Democrat *and* a Christian or Jew. Well, I suppose you could, but it would look hypocritical since the platforms and agendas of the Democratic Party are not only non-Christian and non-Jewish, they are founded in Marxism (or fascism, or communism, or whatever). This statement does *not* give any other political party a pass. Most Republicans in office are RINO's, *Republicans-in-name-only*, and are on-board with all the Marxist-Fascist-Communist crap. It is just that the donkey party is in your face with their agendas. Independents are not much better either. People who are part of this problem *can* change... or, as "they" say, "clean up their act."

I suppose that if those hateful slugs had some decent examples to compare themselves to, "it" might not be so bad. For now, anyway, try looking to the Libertarian Party, the Tea Party, or any person or party that shows some *Constitutionality.* Getting the "true facts" can be a real chore, so don't just accept any dribble someone is handing you. Everything has a price, so you have to ask yourself, "who does this idea *benefit,* how high is the *cost* (sacrifice) and *who* pays?"

Many people hassle other people with their petty, offensive and pathetic "right or wrong" *arguments.* I do not want to hear, and could care less, about the emotional dribble people dream up to argue about. Maybe some true facts about the issue with an intelligent and logical plan to discuss that SACRIFICE would go a long way. Hmmm... I guess we just took the liberal/democrat/communist component out of the picture, huh? Is this Factoid Conduct?

CHAPTER 15

LEADERSHIP

As you leave your past, proceeding into the future, in search of success and promise… people from all walks of life are watching you… literally. They may even be recording your moves with today's advanced surveillance toys that anyone can buy and use. Science is great stuff until you have to defend a particular Conduct someone has recorded and taken public. This is no laughing matter. Small things become big things when your company and family fall apart over some gesture or action that a mean, despicable person has recorded and used against you.

It is best to be a Leader in life. Leaders set the trend for the followers. Leaders have a special important edge over non-leaders. Leaders of one group can interface with leaders of another group and cause change. Depending on the forum, these changes can be huge. Leaders have another important edge – they can hold themselves distant from, or immune to, the very changes they are making for others.

Whether leading your team on the factory floor, or leading your team on the playground, you get first dibs on the water fountain.

Leaders have the right and power to make certain decisions and usually are well compensated *for* those decisions. A leader does not necessarily have to be on location to make important decisions, either. They can delegate that authority to someone else and create another leader. Leaders can earn favor from subordinates by relinquishing their own position in the "water line." They can allow certain behaviors that are outside of pro-tocol. They have an excellent position for covering up mistakes, or making mistakes on purpose to achieve some end. Leaders might be admired for accomplishment by people who are in a position to reward them in ways having nothing to do with company profit. They can accept or refuse anything falling under, or near their purview. They can cause comfort or con-flict for anyone near them. Leaders can be good or bad. They can be in leadership by election, appointment, choice or force and they can make demands of others without their permis-sion. Although it would be nice to be a leader who is liked by subordinates and associates, pleasing everybody in not going to happen and it is not required. As a leader, you can crush and reward at will. Let your grounding and conscience be your guide and be a Good Leader. That's an order, Skippy! How is *that* for Good Conduct?

Conduct

Depending on the group size, leadership and pecking order can be a fun study. It can be in the company office, the factory floor, the card-playing club, family reunion, churches, grocery lines, etc. You might be surprised at who floats to the top in various groups. Some leadership positions are safe, most are not. I cannot include the leadership of any government, because to include the words "leadership" and "government" in the same line, by today's standards is an oxymoron.

If you are a leader, you are going encounter a lot of personal opposition. It makes little difference what you are leading... someone wants your chair or wants to see you fail and sometimes they go to extraordinary lengths to that end. Watch your back, and... never forget the politics and agendas. Remember, a leader of bag people in the storm-sewer system is still a leader.

Leadership might be considered *directing for change*. In business and industry, that *change* is meant to provide *profit*. In politics, it means whatever they can get away with. Lovely, huh?

Do not look for any leadership to come from a politician. Almost all the politicians are polished liars and do not *lead* anything. They promote and press *agendas* - their own and those of their handlers. If I am expected to look to the White House occupant as the "leader of the free world," I should have one of those cookie-tossing bags from an airplane seat... I suppose you could call that *reactionary* Conduct.

Let us check in with a mighty Leader and magnificent military man to hear what he had to say in the Michigan legislature, in Lansing, Michigan on May 15, 1952 –

Talk of imminent threat to our national security through the application of external force is pure nonsense. Our threat is from the insidious forces working from within which have already so drastically altered the character of our free institutions --- those institutions we proudly called the American way of life.

— General Douglas MacArthur (1880 – 1964)

Do you understand what he said in 1952? It is a powerful message describing our demise from within. There is not going to be a conquering band of rogues assaulting our shores. The conquering rogues are in the Capital Building. Political "Leadership"... ugh! Are you able to see my point?

CHAPTER 16

AUTHORITY

Be careful about confusing leadership with *authority*. It happens frequently, but it may not be right, and there are some hurt feelings and bloody noses out there to prove it. Then again, there is the problem of people in authority who give themselves the self-appointed rank of leader, and nobody is challenging their self-assigned "leadership." I will try to give an example of what I mean.

The *leader* might be a president of a company who built the business from the ground up, hired his people, and gives them direction. Although that president could just as well have been hired by a board of directors, he is still the leader. As leader, the president will appoint or hire people for positions of *authority*, such as an accountant who is not expected to lead anybody, but has the *authority* to balance the books, deal with the bank, and prepare paychecks.

A person with *authority* who is *also* in the position of *leadership* might be illustrated by a Pastor, Priest, Rabbi, Spiritualist or who- ever. Followers have given these people the *authority* to *lead* them through their spiritual needs. Anyway, you get the idea.

Next is my idea of a glaring and disgusting example of people who have *authority* and seize the position of *leadership* with *nobody's per- mission* and proceed to openly and intentionally corrupt the sub- ordinates they are leading - I'll take on public "education" and school teachers for this one... including administrators and board members.

As I said a little earlier, "government" and "leadership" are two words that do not belong in the same line, plot or discussion. In the public classroom, we are right back to politics and agendas with *some* of those so-called "teachers" shrinking the heads of our children to hammer home their own political ideologies, sacrilege and stupid opinions. Worse, the whole group is being swept into central government control of curriculum, rules and compliance, forcing exceptional performers and poor performers to co-exist in the same areas and be subjected to intellectual immersion of radi- cal and irresponsible subject matter. This anti-American agenda is coming out of Washington, DC and the National Education Association (NEA). It is rubber-stamped by school boards and administrators.

If the material were based on the time-proven lessons about read- ing, writing, arithmetic and civics, which include the Bill of Rights and the U.S. Constitution, this subject would be a non-issue. But no – once again special interest is holding sway with the young and vulnerable minds of our children. Here is the way I see it: ALL public teachers are guilty. They are paying their dues to their local and/or national union (NEA), or supporting the people who are. They are all on board with the Communist Party to corrupt the children – right out of the Karl Marx Communist Manifesto. Do I sound as if I am generalizing and sweeping everyone in public schools into the same pile? You got THAT right! Whether you, *the teacher,* like it or not, you are guilty by association... literally. Indifferent and complicit administrators and board members are all equally guilty.

I know there are wonderful, conscientious, thoughtful, loving, well-meaning people in the public education system. Where is the voice on the government "education" dole that will openly condemn the direction public education is going? I hope this trend reverses soon. I have serious issues with some about their image, intellect and compensation too. Those topics will have to wait and be addressed in another speech.

Of course, there is another built-in problem with most public school districts - they promote from within, meaning the lousy teachers become lousy principals. There were some really good administrators in the not-to-distant past, but the PCS (politically correct syndrome) now prevails to the total exclusion of responsible and proper Conduct – think agenda, power, fear and zero tolerance. The weak teacher deals with classroom problems by screaming about the "sky falling" and gets the administration involved, who also are weak. Now it is cops, newspapers, finger pointing, counselors and on and on. Then, of course, we have all the lazy, lousy non-parents who want someone else to watch their poorly raised and/or now-criminal kids, and... It gets worse, but I will stop here, for now. Phew, man... how about some *good* news?

Okay, good news. I hereby appoint you to make a positive change. Fair?

Some graduates looking for jobs, have the school system for future employment. I imagine some of you have your own idea of what public schools ought to be. Go after it and have a ball... with Good Conduct.

CHAPTER 17

FOLLOWERS

Most people who are not leaders are followers... sort of. They are following somebody or something, somewhere.

People of great accomplishment follow their instincts; everybody else follows orders or examples.

Some folks follow news stories to lost mines and sunken treasure, or to drilling rigs, or to business and industry of some sort. Government workers follow the examples of other government workers and do... well... you tell me. Maybe that is *reflective* Conduct.

You can be a successful follower and, frankly, should be. A good follower is leading other people somewhere. Follow the line to the diploma, and then follow the right people to more education and contacts leading you to wealth, happiness, admiration, and recognition. That is the Conduct you need. Follow the leader to the pot of gold. Be aware – someone training a follower will want the chosen follower to succeed. It is in their genes and should be in yours. A good follower will target the leader's seat. A good leader will sense it and help to that end.

Then, of course, there are the anal, territorial followers (or, "leaders") who will abuse the very people who have to follow *them*. Disgruntled followers can be a force to be reckoned with. The history books are filled with stories of once-great leaders who screwed their followers and ended in defeat. Too bad. Nobody wants to be a losing follower under bad leadership. Happens all the time. Your leader is following orders of his leader, who is following... I think you get the picture. We are all following... then come the agendas, which can be good or bad.

Unfortunately, for most of us, any agenda is usually bad. Could be as simple as a factory supervisor (a higher-up follower) allowing so-called "harmless" little breaches of established policy to gain favor with one or a few employees. On a grand scale, it might be that of a political agenda that penalizes many good people to gain special-interest favor and, of course, your money.

You will see followers who have no interest in much of anything. I have no idea how they even get to the here-and-now in the first place, but they are here. You may know such a person on a personal level, or know *of* such a person. These folks hire in at the beginners level, never make a peep about anything, usually stay in the background not getting any attention, decline any opportunity to change their status, and then, all of a sudden, retire years later from the same beginner's level. I know of a few folks like that and wonder how their kids turned out. Bummer.

An awful lot of followers, who have to follow a lousy, higher-up follower, will probably be low producers. When you are selecting the group of people to follow you, give a clear understanding of who is in charge and what is expected of everyone, and keep your wishes properly enforced. It will all go a long way towards success.

Good leaders need good followers. The followers support the leaders and everyone involved profits. We are all followers of some sort, so it behooves us to be a *good* follower. More of that Good Conduct.

CHAPTER 18

MISTAKES

Mistakes are going to be made. There are two kinds of mistakes -
yours and theirs. All the fallout of any mistake can be summed up
in a couple of words – who made it and what is the cost?

Some folks call mistakes "accidents." I lean toward calling any mistakes "incidents." I think a good case can be made for identifying
screw-ups as incidents since most so-called "accidents" are *caused*
by someone. Of course, maybe the curve in the road is to blame
for the "accident" caused by some moron driving too fast. It might
be an accident if it is a rockslide crushing the poor people below
(accidental death?) … or windblown collapses, etc.

As far as *who* makes the mistake, it can go to an individual or a
group of individuals. An individual can cheerfully confess or
blame someone or some*thing* else. Mistakes can be cheap or

horribly expensive. A cheap mistake might be that of some poor slob bare-handing the lid on a pot of boiling water – painful, but not horrible. An expensive mistake might be in ignoring important advice – as in icebergs and sinking the Titanic.

A mistake several folks make is holding another person or people to a Secret Standard. Here we have very innocent players finding themselves accused, and even punished, for violating some rule or confidence they were not aware of. The old "ignorance of the law" baloney does not gain play here.

Rules are in place for a reason. If the rules are in written form and are a formal policy, then anyone who is privy to any knowledge or actions conducted under those circumstances is bound by those rules – which include confidentiality and behavior of all manner. Make sure everyone involved is aware of the rules, whether they are getting a forklift license or the combination to the door of King Solomon's mines. Same goes for any gathering where the people involved have *implied* rules and the information is private. Areas affected might include company secrets of research and development, family medical problems, commodity trades and so on.

These rules are broken all the time. People get into gatherings, have a few drinks, engage in a conversation and whoops! Shouldn't have said *that*. Too late now. Better tell someone of the breach and get some damage control going. Of course, being a traitor and spying are big business. Secrets are bartered as a means to money, revenge, ideology or personal power all the time. Don't forget those agendas folks. The power of information, or the lack of it, is well established. Liars are brokering information constantly for nothing more than some favor with the opposite sex.

Conduct

Politicians are notorious for "leaking" so-called *secret* information – usually to drive their agenda somewhere. So, what about those *Secret* Standards?

Violators of Secret Standards will be falsely accused on purpose, not by mistake. Secret standards arise when a person or people share information with others who simply do not know the information is privileged for one reason or another. The person giving up the information does not know there is another or others who are in a position to become aware of such information. The speaker's mistake. As long as everyone keeps his or her lips sealed, no harm. Seldom works that way. For some, to be given a hot little morsel of information with no stated restriction is as good as a winning poker hand. The agenda game is on with these folks. Nevertheless, there are those who come into the information and freely discuss it with others, not realizing the info was intended to be kept private. Too bad. Now the dope who leaked the story goes after the poor guy who repeated it, and openly accuses that person of bad Conduct. This type of persecution can become a major self-defense issue. It has placed the good guy in the terrible position of proving the bad guy a liar. That is one example of the Secret Standard.

There is another devious wrinkle to this type of Conduct – that of being accused of a certain behavior for no apparent reason whatsoever. The intent here is to degrade, reduce or neutralize your ability to make a case for some pending or future issue or cause. This is an old political trick that may be new to you. The struggle for power and favor causes a lot of grief. In office politics, you may be accused, discussed and found guilty of a non-existent issue – all behind your back. In public *and* private office, character assassination is routine business. However, it can, and usually does, get worse. Mistakes in this arena can be real shockers. Now that you have been falsely accused and found guilty in the court of public or private opinion, where do you go? Who is in a position to help you? Who actually cares enough to get involved in your situation when their own ass might go *on the line*? Do you do anything at all? Do you fall to pieces and hope it all goes away? Well folks, meet the Eighty-Twenty Rule. When you are down and out, looking for help, eighty per cent of the people do not care, and the other twenty per cent are glad it happened to you. Sorry, but sometimes the good guys come in last. Plenty has been written and spoken about why bad things happen to good people.

The Secret Standard phenomenon has risen to a new, sinister, deliberate, *and* dangerous stage as of late. Federal politicians, judges and agencies are writing illegal laws in secret and compelling various secret agencies and people to enforce them. Not good folks. You can be seized, secluded, imprisoned or murdered, with no warrant, reason or explanation from anyone. All you know is that you have been accused of breaking some vague law virtually no one outside of the secret circle knows. This issue rides right along with secret agendas of politicians who will go to any length to "get their way." Remember that *Tyranny*? This holds you and me to standards we have no idea even exist, and those standards are specifically for the benefit of a very select "someone else." So much for democracy, let alone our wonderful, former Republic. NDAA (National Defense Authorization Act)… it is bad… *very* bad.

The "collateral damage" that can come from all this might require a new definition. I often wonder how many innocent people in buildings, planes, boats and more, have been collaterally maimed and murdered in the quest to stop information from being made public or to set the stage for more draconian laws, rules and orders. Looks like False Flags folks... Bad Conduct by bad people. Mistake? I doubt it!

I often wonder if anyone is ever going to be punished for any of those "mistakes?" Just another one of those brain-fart questions, Lucy.

CHAPTER 19

LUCK

Luck is what happens when preparation meets opportunity.
- Lucius Annaeus Seneca (4BC – 65AD)

The word "Luck" can probably be defined as "an occurrence of chance that might go in your favor, or might not." That said, I suppose we have now set the stage for "good" Luck, or "bad" Luck. We can now have other factors play into our Luck, such as karma, or extra sensory perception, and maybe spiritualism, seers and psychics.

As long as intelligence has been around, people have been trying to improve their chances in life using just about every conceivable mix of apparent nonsense they can dream up. There are so many methods employed by so many people, a complete detail of the subject is beyond the scope of this presentation. However, the people who study and use these methods are believers and passionate about those beliefs. You might see some strange Conduct in these circles. I wouldn't want to be the one caught swiping anybody's special bones, teeth, cards, crystal balls, rocks, tea leaves, cups, bowls, gems, Ouija boards... or... well... I think you see where I'm going here. Anyway, we really need to ask the question, "Can these beliefs and practices be parlayed into some sort of a change in chance or Luck?" Well, the answer is probably subjective, but most likely, folks who have tried and succeeded will swear *by* it, and those who have tried and failed will swear *at* it. Since I'm doing the talking here, I will tell you I have studied this phenomena most of my adult life and as far as I am concerned, it appears to be very real and definitely works for some people. I am not a practitioner of such Conduct, but the evidence seems to be quite extensive in favor of it. I have been in the presence of people who seemed to have some amazing abilities, whereby they did not know me from Adam, but provided private information about me no one else could or would have known. I have also been flat-out instantly changed from one state of existence to another. Whether any of this is Supernatural or Unnatural, I have no idea, but I lean toward the Supernatural since the results and occurrences I am privy to, have been positive.

There will never be any substitute for hands-on, educated labor to achieve a specific end. Whether that labor is building pyramids or launching rockets, somebody had to come up with the idea and cause a directed workforce to *do* something.

From time to time, we hear of some laboratory that got "Lucky" and developed a special life-saving drug, or maybe a botanist discovers some life-saving plant in the middle of nowhere, seemingly by total accident. A very thin *maybe* for Luck or chance of these occurrences since the stage was set for some sort of discovery in the first place. How about the person who is in the mountains looking for gold and trips on an outcrop of rich ore? Is that Luck? Hard to say – that is why the person was there to begin with.

These so-called discoveries are sidebars of hard work... or are they? What if the folks making these discoveries had consulted a seer or psychic of some sort for guidance on where to be and what to see? Is it still Luck, now? Hiking with the kids and finding a vein of gold might be luck.

How about a chance meeting in a busy airport with a complete stranger who can tell you what kind of sickness you have and how to deal with it... still Luck? How about the psychic healers who have a record of accomplishment in diagnoses and cures? Or the Astrological mapping and associated predictions that happen? Did you get "Lucky" with a new partner last night?

Luck is what you make it, but remote viewing is a science and it is real. History tells us that a fellow named Nostradamus (1503 – 1566) gazed into a bowl of water and accomplished an astonishing track record of correct predictions. Many people believe his predictions and prophecies are still being fulfilled. Edgar Cayce (1877 – 1945) was a trance-state psychic, who is credited with correctly calling racetrack winners consistently, as well as making numerous predictions about topics such as Atlantis, the pyramids and medicine. There are plenty more, but I think you see where all this can go.

Purveyors of Luck and chance are both real and phony. The history books are full of all manner of men and women who made a tidy sum of money through elaborate schemes to defraud customers looking for a shortcut to fame and fortune. The fakes and phonies are the ones who make the most rag copy or talk-show discussion. I suppose you could say that the poor slobs who lost the money experienced bad Luck. The *real* ones are those who you may never ever meet or even hear about. Finding a person who can actually make a change in your life using what I call *unnatural methods* can take a great deal of effort. I say, "unnatural" to make the distinction from "Supernatural," which is generally taken to have Divine implications. Maybe they go together (?). Supernatural occurrences are very definitely real and happen quite frequently. Instantaneous healings take place all over the world and are part of Supernatural Conduct, which calls upon God to make a change. I have seen it, experienced it, and it is real.

There are many well-documented cases of people from the "other side" who have made contact with the *here and now*. These cases include contacts where the "spirits" or ghosts can give irrefutable confirmation of who they are, where they have been and who they know in the after-life realm as well as in the current physical realm. Sometimes these entities can make accurate predictions, and other times they will tell us they cannot see the future. I have studied many cases of this apparent unnatural contact and few can say anything accurate about lotteries, horse races and the like. Some are extraordinarily proficient about the past – both recent and ancient. They can provide details that only an experienced and knowledgeable scientist can, and usually does, confirm. The subjects discussed can range from buried treasure to star travel. These unnatural happenings are real, folks. Chances are you have been witness to one or more and did not know it. I guarantee you, any sane person employing unnatural means to any wealth or fame, sure-as-the-world ain't gonna' tell *you* about it. You might see the results, but few brag, and that is as good as it gets.

However, the subject here is Luck. How about *your* Luck? Can you rattle any marbles or do any card pitching to change your own prospects of wealth and fame? Can you learn any tidbits of information that might result in some "Lucky" change in your future? Coming from me, the short answer is "yes." People needing water can find someone to dowse for it. There are some remarkable stories of people who read Tarot Cards. Years ago, I was taught how to prepare a deck of playing cards and read them. It works. I do, however, think there might have been some divine help on that one... or some remarkable Luck.

Luck occurs in strange ways. Good Luck takes real work. Bad Luck is simple. I will stick to the good Luck. So, now what?

Well, this paper is about Conduct, so any change in your Luck means you have to Conduct yourself accordingly. You need to decide what kind of changes you want to implement. Do you want to change the weather? That might not qualify as Luck and require a request to the Indians about a tribal rain dance. Would you like to dangle a pendulum and find an oil field or have those winning lottery numbers picked out for you? You may want to decide if all the effort, *and it is a lot of effort,* is worth going up against nature. We are talking about some serious and impressive forces here. Any change you may elicit will likely not be obvious. It is at this point you need to shift focus over to what you are willing to risk. Some folks pull it off without a hitch. Others fall into dark depths of human misery. They get sidetracked and suddenly want to be a white or black witch. Conduct yourself extremely carefully when entering into the unnatural.

Picking *out* a particular unnatural discipline probably comes first. Getting in touch with a practitioner of the art you are interested in might be a place to start. Of course, now you have an excellent opportunity to experience Bad Luck.

You could go with crystal gazing. Plenty has been written about this discipline from ancient times to the present. I thought I wanted to read crystal balls and amassed a rather large collection of writings as well as a large collection of crystal balls. I still have both collections, but never got around to trying it out. Now I just call them spirit-world marbles… big ones.

The types and compositions of various crystals and crystal balls are huge. The balls require special handling and the gazer, or *scryer,* needs special preparations for any meaningful results. Therefore, I recommend that any new student do the necessary research for the proper preparation and practice of this Conduct. Same goes for automatic writing, speaking and so forth. Like I said, "it is real work," and few are up to it. Nevertheless, *preparation and opportunity* is "out there."

I will say one more thing on this topic – there are a couple of types of crystal balls – leaded glass balls and mineral balls, which may, or may not, be clear. The clear mineral balls are the "real ones" in some circles. Good balls take good money, and the mineral balls are available in all types of minerals that are pretty, but not necessarily clear. Regardless of which ball you end up with, if you plan to scry it, do this: Don't touch it. Pick it up and handle it with a clean cloth until you find out why. If it is going to be a conversation piece, don't worry about it. You can always start with the water bowl.

Since we are in this unnatural material, I might add this: I have seen a person effect a change on another person with an amazing result. It is as if one person "zapped" the other. Weird.

In the event you should decide to try this Conduct for your amusement, I would recommend being on the *right* side with God. Beats me if that is possible, but if you were a clairvoyant, you would know... maybe.

Hey! Maybe you have a brilliant future of wealth and fame reading broken sticks and dog hair! After all, some folks pay well to see weird people in cone-shaped hats with colored stars, just to predict their future! More of that *Preparation and opportunity,* folks.

Never easy, is it?

CHAPTER 20

RESPECT

This is an important Conduct where people recognize certain particular attributes of other people, customs, places, things and whatnot. In the "whatnot" department, we might show respect for anything from making room for another person in a wheelchair, to avoiding bare electrical wires, or maybe a hot stove. What about a crazy person with a rock pick? How about some respect for an important politician, performer, scientist, religious person and more.

Of course, what conversation about respect would be complete without reference to *disrespect*? We probably see more of this than the good kind. Instead of seeing reverence for something or some-one, now we see contempt. I must say, "A lot of people deserve it!" As a matter-of-fact, some people say that other people deserve so much disrespect they *just need killing*. Boy!! Now there is a red hot button that covers a lot of ground. Don't take it too lightly – a lot of people believe it. You hear me? A *lot*! And that, ladies and gentlemen, take us into the morality zone.

It seems as if many folks are running out of places to go – go to get away from all the immorality, profanity and vulgarity being shoved in their face every day by all means – TV, movies, politicians, political action groups, people on the street, in stores, in restaurants and on and on. The perps will keep pushing, shoving and annoying until someone hits the wall. Nowhere to go. Now then, what is all that about a cornered and mad rabid animal? However, I digress.

In a column under the word "respect," we find a whole lot of vocabulary. Certainly, *Conduct* is high on that list. *Trust* might be next. If I can Trust people to Conduct themselves appropriately in my space, the case is closed. For the most part, a few years back and on back to the beginning of our Republic, that *is* how it *was*. Not so anymore. If we have anything left after the government is done with us, seems like many other people are trying to strip us even more. Rodney Dangerfield covered it well with his phrase, "I don't get no respect." I'd better watch it. There might be people out there who have no idea who Rodney Dangerfield is (a comedian who died in 2004).

There was a day when respect could be taken for granted. People did not "sass" their elders or people of obvious authority, and treated each other as they would want to be treated… the Golden Rule, if you will. Seemed like most folks had a job, a home, a car and plenty to eat. Kids played, laughed, ate watermelon in the back yard, spit seeds at each other and had real fun. I don't know about you, but I don't see a whole lot of that anymore. Surely, it is out there. Neighbors were included in picnics and helped each other with all kinds of repairs and upkeep. There was mutual understanding of need, pain, help and privacy. There was good, juicy gossip from time-to-time, and those involved were discreet with the news. There was more smiling, waving and general friend-liness toward each other. Negative, grumpy people were openly told to cheer up and share, or shed, their concerns. People cared about each other. They had a genuine interest in the well-being of folks around them. People seemed to have fundamental wis-dom and knew if news was bad it probably hurt. They were more careful about repeating bad news and if the news was repeated, at least the story was not radically changed for shock factor. People with deformities, infirmities and impediments garnered proper respect and were treated with the proper dignity. Everybody knew a little something about several subjects and could sustain an intel-ligent conversation regardless of their age. There was a great deal of mutual respect. Stories were swapped, dreams were discussed, plans were made, projects got started and progress was made. A lot of Good Conduct taking place.

Things are vastly different now-a-days. The special interest groups and un-American Constitution-hating politicians have invaded your lives with such vigor and violence, you have few "rights," few people you can trust with anything... little, if any, infrastructure to settle concerns of any manner, and zero privacy. Worse, the government infrastructure has become a force that subjectively decides if your formerly private speech, writings, or shopping interests should be a reason to prosecute you. The government is telling your neighbors to spy on you and report any "suspicious behavior" to the "authorities." Who in hell is any neighbor to make *those* kinds of judgments? Or anybody at all for that matter. Now your Conduct is open to review and condemnation by any creep who wants to make your life miserable. To say that the government affords the citizens *no respect* is a gross, flaming understatement. Worse, the main-stream-media gives them cover.

The old saying, "bad news travels like wildfire," is a small match for the saying, "crap rolls downhill." It starts on Capitol Hill, goes down from there, and gets profoundly worse. Maybe it is time to *groom* that "hill." I am open to ideas. I will respect anything you say... or think.

Be kind to your fellow man, if you can. Move through life with proper speech, poise and presence. Excel at all you can. Doors will open for you. Life can still be good. Be a volunteer for folks needing some sort of help, and assist others with mentoring, tutoring and friendship. Try to interface with other people and broaden your base of knowledge and theirs too.

The Boy Scout motto is BE PREPARED which means the Scout is always in a state of readiness in mind and body to do his DUTY. As an adult, in these trying times, I would add *to* that Mind and Body with gold, silver, currency, food, fuel, water, guns and ammo. Prepare for yourself since no one else is going to do it for you. It will show self-respect, respect for loved ones and be Good Conduct.

The current political climate should have your attention and when the collapse comes, you will have few, if any, friends. *Former* friends and legions of everyone else will come for your "stuff." You will be part and parcel to new levels of disrespect.

CHAPTER 21

MILITARY

Of all the things we need as a nation, a good, solid, respectful and ready military machine is right up there at the top of the list. It seems as if we have one. The ground troops I see and hear about are a special group of supermen and I deeply respect them. After all, who else would sign a blank check made out to the government and honor it with their limbs and lives?

Of all the things we do not need, it seems to me, are more "armchair generals." As far as I am concerned, most of the great generals have come and gone. The big military boots-on-the-ground campaigns with legions of men at arms being directed by mighty military men of strength and Character are a bygone era. It also seems like a *few* of the active-duty generals and admirals I see today are armchair cowards tail-piping a suspicious commander-in-chief (president??). We are burdened with a chief-of-staff over a cabal of "czars," also known as the *presidential cabinet* (more tail-piping yes-men) who take pleasure in dreaming up ways for stripping American Citizens of any rights and dignity, all the while coming up with means of punishment for non-compliance with their plethora of government edicts. To say we have a commander-in-chief over that staff chief, is about equal to saying we have something needing a flush. What poor slob would willingly salute *something needing a flush*, and do it in public? A shameful collection of self-serving despots bent on absolute power and control over everything known to man. Of course, they are able to run roughshod over everyone because the Capital Building is full of congressional liars, cowards, crooks and communists refusing to uphold the Constitution of the United States.

I know there are really good generals "out there" who are more than worthy of the respect and admiration afforded (or denied) them. I am sure they are groaning in disbelief at how "things" are going, as well. I am also painfully aware that numerous General, Flag and Field Officers are being muzzled, reprimanded and fired for showing any disagreement with the criminals in the White House and capitol building. A few who try to speak out are denied any forum by main-stream-media, or threatened by politicians. Worse, the enlisted troops who serve under these officers are bound by the same edicts. Hmmm... isn't there some sort of Constitutional remedy for all of our ills? No help from the punks in Congress... Ugh!

I imagine there is more groaning going on "in the ranks" as the geniuses-in-charge fill up the military with muslims and then capitulate to muslim demands for freedom to do as they wish with respect to our formerly traditional military dress code and code of Conduct. Of course we wouldn't want to forget about the muslim in Texas who was an Army officer and murdered thirteen and wounded 30 more of our troops all in the name of allah[2] (Nidal Hasan, Fort Hood, TX, November 5, 2009). Unbelievably, that act of outright hate and terror had been classified as workplace violence. I would also imagine there is a lot of groaning going on in the various alphabet agencies as the guy in the White House loads up our "national security" with more islamics[3] of known enemy association. This same guy wants to reduce our military strength to pre-WW II levels... as the world falls apart because of U.S. of A. involvement around the globe... which has no importance to anyone but the cabal inside the beltway. Sure does look like they are just destroying what was *there* and promoting the expansion of enemy strength for their own amusement – which "we the people" will live to regret for many generations hence.

I am picking on a *small few* people with stars, bars and stripes here... I also know there are plenty of wonderful men and women in the *entire* officer corps and enlisted ranks.

Where are the "great people" leading the charge for peace and freedom? Probably retired or dead. Who would *want* to lead a bunch of Patriots into a conflict having nothing to do with the United States' best interest, under the direction of a... well, time to clamp it, again. Just another routine military loss.

You realize I am just rendering an opinion here, but there are mountains of facts and evidence to make my case. If you have any doubts here, please do your research as I did!

---

2 Lower case intentional
3 Ibid

How about those women in the military? Let me see if I have this right – we take young, healthy, virile men who are reaching testosterone peaks and then train these men to fight to the death for some vague cause. During this training, they are instructed in the glory of country and corps giving them a sky-high ego. Next, we turn them over to a unit where the training and egos are shared, strengthened, and sharpened. Now these young, powerful men are brainwashed into thinking the war they about to engage in is for some nefarious good of our country. *Then...* some "brilliant" political dumbass places a bunch of young menstruating-age women-in-uniform right in the midst of these fighting men, and then actually expect everybody to keep their pants *zipped*?! Worse, a high percentage of the women wind up pregnant, giving us force of broken hearts and grief, instead of a force for battle. Give me a break... where on earth do these morons-in-charge come from?

I got news for ya' folks... as a Marine in the Viet Nam War, I saw many GI's dealing with the testosterone alarm, and it sure helped those guys to have a women turn that alarm off. Another great day for condoms, huh?

I suppose military queers and dykes chase each other... OOPS! Did that slang offend anyone? I hope not. Bummer... Is it time to get mad, swear, and yell out dirty names? Have we a hateful troublemaker looking for some sort of recognition?! I wonder what kind of Conduct THAT is?! I am very sick and tired of having homo behavior and agendas shoved in my face, day in, and day out! Maybe the America-haters stumping for the gay/les cause are worse (?) Listen folks, if you all with the same-sex attractions want to "do your thing," remember – you comprise a miniscule piece of the population and involve yourselves in Conduct that is abhorrent to most of the rest. Please find Jesus or go back in the closet. All my excellent opinion for thought, of course.

We certainly would not want to forget about the demoralizing destruction of great military, all-men institutions of higher learning forced to accept women that could not "hack it," all in the name of "political correctness." I know there are good military women in the ranks. So, I have to ask, "When are they going to put on the armor and charge the enemy?" Generalizing is always risky...

After my stint in Viet Nam, I started looking for reasons why anyone would do such a lousy job of Conducting a war. I found out. Same reason the Korean Conflict was lost as well as every military involvement since. Those wars were lost on purpose to feed cash and conversation into the smoking lounges and egos of the political/industrial/military crooks who want to run the world as their own private playground. You think I am kidding? Look at the mess our so-called "leaders" have "led" us into! Try on crippling debt with massive unemployment... gutted retirement, savings, and investment accounts... real estate values in the toilet... skyrocketing inflation and living costs... add to all of that our crippled and dead military warriors... massive separation of classes... a burdened middle class, private-sector paying all the bills for everything - submarines, space programs, wars, welfare... government employees with disproportionate wages and salaries... and, oh yeah... merging us into a world government (the UN) of more despots. Are they for real?! You can bet your ass they are for real. And, of course, those tailpipe officers. As near as I can tell, those people are training the military in such a fashion that, for people like me to be a patriotic, flag-waving proud citizen is becoming a crime. I imagine that I am not too far out when I suppose there are a *few generals, and/or others* who want to train the troops to fire upon U.S. Citizens too, huh? Waco, Texas, April 19, 1993, was "training 101." All those tailpipe presidential appointees giving all those illegal orders that ignored the Posse Comitatus Act of 1878, and working hard to criminalize Christianity makes a body wonder. I could be wrong about all of this, but the "beltway" Conduct bears me out. They love the NDAA of 2012, which stripped away rights of the U.S. citizen, neutered Posse Comitatus and every other Constitutional *protection from* the "Fed." People in my age group (mid 60's) can see this - if they even care. Younger folks may not know anything different. Anyway, my offer still stands – *prove me wrong.*

Since I am on this subject, let's take a minute or two to talk about all those military weapons, vehicles and tactical support gear being handed over to local police. Looks like a military police force to me. If those towns and cities accepted all that equipment from the federal government, then it stands to reason, the feds want something in return. Of course they do... the feds want all police to be *federal* police taking orders from the central government in Washington D C. Your police chief and elected sheriff will be taking orders from afar. Man... some Conduct there, huh?! Golly bum, Mack... I wonder who pays for all of that??

So, how does all this fit into a presentation about Conduct? Just about every way possible. You and I are being manipulated into accepting whatever the central regime doles out. The central regime *creates problems* and then assigns legions of federal employees, contractors, agents and *armies* to carry out the central-regime cure for the *previously non-existent* problems.

Conduct

Notice how the current president is making up law and has involved himself in local police issues from North to South. This Conduct softens up the populace to accept presidentially directed (micromanaged) federal involvement in local and all issues. The feds under the current president have openly, politically attacked individual States over local jurisdictional issues, forcing massive failures and/or crippling slow-downs in the state and local political systems.

Back to those military folks in uniform. The men and women in uniform, in the field, fighting the wars with their actions restricted and/or outright compromised, have my undying gratitude. I know in my heart those great men and women are doing all that they *can* or, are *allowed* to do. I also know they all are a proud bunch deserving of the highest recognition. I hope those folks know some general out there somewhere to whom they can look up and admire.

If anyone likes watching movies, and in this case, military movies, remember – the players are *actors* following a *script* under a *director*. A lot of the writing is outright fabrication and misplaced information, all tailored to *shrink your head*. Of course, movies are for the entertainment value, but the writers, actors and directors can send you a message. You paid the money, and *they* are going to get *your* money's worth. Movies can still be fun to watch.

If you saw the movie *PATTON* (1970), starring George C. Scott, you may remember a line he recited – *"No bastard ever won a war by dying for his country, He won it by making the other poor dumb bastard die for his country."* That might be a cleaned-up (made-up?) variation of a speech given June 5, 1944 by the late, great, General George S. Patton, Jr. His troops got the messages loud and clear with plenty of expletives for emphasis… and they went on to do a mighty fine job!

But, what about all the people who actually *believe* misleading movies? Seems like a bunch of movie-making folks are counting on low-information viewers. I suppose since you can't cross-examine a movie, it eliminates that intellectual challenge, huh? Still entertaining though.

Since I am talking about Patton, I will add this - the circumstances surrounding his death are very suspicious. It looks as if he had an important message for us and some politicos wanted him silenced.

We have wonderful military fighting forces. I just wish those forces could be put to use *Constitutionally*. We would be much better off and it would be Good Conduct.

> *May God have mercy upon my enemies, because I won't.*
>   General George S. Patton, Jr. (1885 – 1945)

> *No man is entitled to the blessings of freedom unless he be vigilant in its preservation.*
>   General Douglas MacArthur (1880 – 1964)

When asked about forgiving the enemy –

> *I believe that forgiving them is God's function. Our job is simply to arrange the meeting.*
>   General H. Norman Schwarzkopf, Jr. (1934 – 2012)

Many powerful, wonderful warriors from the Marines, Navy, Army and Air Force have come, gone, and are here today. Fat chance we will again see them in any meaningful action anytime soon.

CHAPTER 22

PLAN

Conducting your affairs and your life with some sort of fore-thought and direction will help keep you on track to a specific goal... in other words, a Plan.

The loss of time, money and accomplishment living a reactionary life style are incalculable.

The pages of history are replete with stories of people who seemingly possessed few articles of value, had average employment, lived in a modest home complete with a family and yet upon death, leave an enormous estate. So, how did they do it? Simple – they had a Plan and stayed focused on it. Let me restate that - they had a Plan and stuck to it.

There are also the obvious indicators of people who Planned, stayed with that Plan, and have the trappings and lifestyle to prove it.

Having a Plan is a major part of the equation. However, conviction to follow through on that Plan is the rest of the equation.

Generally, weak personalities make weak players in life. Those who go through life without a goal and no Plan are governed by circumstance and the will of others. Keep this type of person at a distance. You will know them by several identifying characteristics. One of the clue's might be that of someone who has little personal wealth, has no desire to improve, is perfectly content with their situation and comes to you looking for a job... Hmmm... maybe a dab of "loser repellant" would be good.

The list of detrimental and negative attributes that some people carry around is very long. It can be collectively called "baggage." This is not to say that all the baggage is bad, but it is very hard to follow any kind of Plan dragging compromising weaknesses along the way. So, this means that having a Plan and sticking to it requires some "backbone" - a strong conviction. It also means that the Plan has a specific goal, and further that people not able to help you accomplish this goal should represent a small number in your circle of friends and associates.

The goal must be realistically attainable and compatible with your chosen life style. It also must remain a secret. Only you should know of your goal unless you can positively identify another person who *can* help you, is willing to do so, and will keep your secret.

I know, I know… if two people know, then it is not a secret. I'll tell ya' folks… the number of people that can be privy to your goal and actually help you is very small.

I am not talking about a construction project involving dozens of others. I am talking about real accomplishment… changes in lives that are positive… beneficial to you and those who you care about. It could be anything from a lifestyle change to amassing great wealth.

One of the ways I like to implement change in my life is to study people who have made similar changes and see what they did. Spare yourself embarrassment and ridicule and keep your ideas to yourself. You know… *do* it! …then talk about it… maybe.

I think several of us know somebody who is a mouthful of "gonna-do's"… I'm gonna' do this, I'm gonna' do that. Pretty tiring, huh?

Remember the old adage, "Be careful what you ask for, you might get it." Trust me, gang - this is one of those activities where "might" becomes "will." Once you form a Plan and put the subconscious into action to achieve that Plan, it is difficult to back out. Again, if it is realistically attainable and compatible, it is a *go*!

Another little tidbit – constant dwelling on any given idea, good or bad, has a strong effect on making those thoughts become action. Once the subconscious notices it, the thought process has begun. There is a Biblical passage about thoughts and actions - *For as he thinketh in his heart, so is he:* (Proverbs 23:7 KJV). The Bible is full of useful ideas and life-encouraging passages. Here is a variant of that Biblical passage from another late, great person -

Whatever the mind can conceive and believe, it can achieve.
                    - Napoleon Hill (1883 – 1970)

How about an *UnPlan*... where someone or something derails your original course of action intentionally; or a natural circumstance... maybe chance? How many times have we heard or said, "I didn't Plan on *that.*" Some people say it so much it appears as if they are living in total confusion. The list of circumstances, events, outcomes and tragedies that we do *not* Plan on can be huge. We do not *Plan* on wrecks, illness, earthquakes, tornadoes, wars, alien invasions, crime, bankruptcy, divorce... or even a winning lottery ticket. Well, you get the idea.

So, since we do not Plan *on* these events, what do we do? We Plan *for* them. I am not suggesting these events will occur, but with some sort of a Plan, we stand a better chance of limiting our losses if they do.

For example - we know our lives will end. With very few exceptions, we do not know when, where or how life will end. However, we can do an estate Plan. We can do an insurance Plan. In other words, we can Plan for a certainty. We can preserve some of what we have worked for and hand off our accomplishments to someone else for their future. (... *Maybe.* The rules on the books now, might be changed later – politics and agendas folks.)

Anyway, I guarantee you – if people have any kind of an estate at all, as a large number of folks do... and they should drop dead without a Plan, they have sentenced their loved ones to a lot of work and loss settling the affairs. This, of course, assumes the decedent did not *intend* to screw them.

Then, there are legions of morons who live below sea level in certain areas near large bodies of water; and of course, we have all the dopes living in valleys under dams of all types. I would not want to forget all those people living on a soft hillside in rainy areas, or in a nice pinewoods waiting for a lightning strike. I realize that most of us do not ride around Planning for a wreck, but if someone wants to gamble that a sure thing will not occur, I hope they have a plan that does not include some sort of government "assistance." Seems like we always have to pay for a lot of counterproductive political involvement of one means or another, which has a glaring track record of making a bad situation profoundly worse. Remember, those government mistakes are not accidents. Just wonderful Conduct all the way around for everybody... right?

In the case of automobile problems, which might lead to property damage or worse, again we have insurance. However, we have more. We can increase our awareness to avoid other drivers, avoid areas known to be problem areas, improve our driving skills, avoid drugs and alcohol... well... you see what I mean.

More un-Planning as in bad luck caused by someone else's dictate, looms over our heads with the politicians changing the medical insurance scheme/scam. This topic is so important you absolutely must research it. Not everyone will need or use Medicaid and medical insurance, but you need to know about how our lovely government is trying desperately to strip out private plans, and how it will affect your future. Government control of medicine and insurance is the final phase for control of you. It sets the stage for denial of everything – from nutritional supplements to banking. Get a Plan now, if *that* is still even *possible*. It ranks right up there with that *death* Plan.

The list of un-Plans is long. Let's take a little look at the "other guys" Plan... The Other Guy's Plan is real, in progress, and planning *for* you, as well as *on* you.

How about your politicians? They have been doing your Planning for a long time. They have drafted people into military service and compelled them to fight needless wars. Of course, someone had to pay for that. So we have been part of someone else's Plan, and subject to their upward spiraling taxes to pay the bill. They Planned all that. Evidently, those politicians find it amusing sending other people off to do their dirty work, becoming crippled or dead, and all the while spending someone else's money to pay for it. Don't you wish you could see some benefit to us for all that expense and carnage?

Your death opens up a completely new library of Plans for everything from your corpse to your living loved ones. You might find it interesting to see the fortunes accumulated for selling a corpse one piece at a time. Yup, just when you thought you had provided science and medicine with a body to study, learn from, and save others, news arrives that the body has become a corpse on a respirator being parted out as needed for profit. I suppose we could call that Big Buck Body Conduct. I hope that someone else is able to go on living with a part or two from your corpse.

Now, finally, your loved ones can continue with settling your estate and paying for funerals, gravesites, headstones, lawyers, accountants and more, trying to preserve that for which you worked so hard to build.

Conduct

How about ideological fanatics? Did you forget the World Trade Center attack of September 11, 2001? And the thousands of lives lost? That attack was just one of many right here on our turf. Entire nations and cultures have been decimated in the name of ideological belief - and those Plans include the United States – you, me and the dog.

The other criminal minds are Planning for you too. Oh boy! Are they ever! If they are not Planning to rape, rob, main and kill you, they might be Planning electronic crime to break you. Professional criminals in the private sector and government want to squeeze more money out of you. They have targeted us with intentional manipulation of stocks & markets, commodities, banking, real estate, dollar worth… anything of any value! Someone, somewhere, is Planning *for* you and Planning *on* you, to wring you out for more cash and compliance. A quick look at some of the asinine laws on the books ought to be a "heads up" that others are happily Planning a dismal future for you and me.

Some of the perpetrators are punished, most are not. Criminals that Plan for you are at all levels of life. They are lurking in the streets. They are working in the office. They are the politicians or your neighbor, spouse or children. Children are experts at manipulating their parents for compliance of their wishes.

Do not forget the financial losses of 2008 to the tune of about 10 Trillion dollars. Who actually did the *losing*? How about all the people who were rewarded for being corrupt, lying, criminals in the money industry around Wall Street, Europe and the entire world? Still going on…

Business and industry is Planning for you, too - everything from garbage to gambling. How about mining, drilling, pipelines, products, pricing, restrictions, transportation, information, housing, and on and on. Numerous huge institutions and government think tanks Plan for and on you... with or without your knowledge or permission.

Oh, yeah! Do not forget about the sex creature out there making a Plan for your significant other! Is your spouse or "friend" wearing that *target*?

I hope you can see where this "Plan thing" is going.

So where do you start? You could start in front of a mirror, take a good, long look, and ask yourself some questions. Questions like, "Am I happy with my life as it is now?" or "If I lose my job tomorrow, do I eat or make car payments?" Or perhaps something like, "If my spouse dropped dead tonight, what becomes of the kids and the house. Am I prepared to buy a funeral, gravesite and headstone?" Or maybe, "What happens if our child contracts some incurable, debilitating and expensive disease?" or, "What if a drunk driver loses control and plows through our house?" Earthquakes, tornadoes and more. These calamities happen every day. Alien invasion??

How about something as in, "What can I do to help a dear friend get through the health, death or divorce crises?" "What do I do when the home loses power in the middle of winter during a heavy blizzard?" "How can I double my income?" or maybe "I want to write a book." How about some other fascination such as racecar driver, shipwreck diver, astronaut, politician, etc., etc.

Conduct

Folks – there are hard realities in life that will force you to face yourself. I cannot tell you what to do when some creep or politician is making your life miserable. I can, however, tell you this, "you may have to take *off* the Good Character jacket and put *on* the hurt-them or kill-them jacket." I think this is another one of those Gray Character areas where an up-standing citizen gets a pass for some not-so-up-standing Conduct. Then again, I reckon you could go on taking it in the butt, or on the other cheek. Back of the head? Bummer... never easy, is it?

What about the Police? Simple – they are people... with friends, families, bosses and maybe driven agendas. I don't know. Pay attention. Someday you might be asked, "What kind of wood is the sawdust between your ears?"

I am finished... for now. You have been a wonderful reader and I appreciate the cheering and clapping for some of my points. I also appreciate those who felt compelled to groan or boo a couple of times. I now say, "Thank you" and I hope to encourage everyone again soon for another installment of my wisdom.

EPILOGUE

Any discussion of Conduct can probably go on forever. In today's declining-of-America, the so-called rules-of-Conduct are becoming pretty much whatever a few people "feel" they ought to be. People who make bad rules that other people must obey, are making yet more rules that increase the difficulty of circumventing the bad ones from the beginning. The bad guys might not *stop* the circumventing, but they will be along soon for the abuse and penalty phase. YOU, the reader, must be aware of what is being done *to* you. Only *you* can do this. There is plenty of opportunity "out there" for the movers and shakers, but it will be by the rules of others. Except for yourself, only precious *few* loved ones and close others can do anything *for* you. Sometimes, like-minded groups can effect some sort of change, but it is difficult. The bad guys are lurking everywhere and they are dealing marked cards with your name on them.

Stay in the proper forums to discuss topics, have your facts right and try to keep a cool head. In all likelihood, you will find small favor for anything you know to be "True Facts." Those folks who *think* they are right, or are *wrong on purpose*, outnumber those folks who truly *are* right. I am absolutely certain that most of the "think-they-are-rights" go along to get along with the rest of the trash. No *ducking* here...

Do your planning as well as you can. If you don't, someone else will.

If you are expected to agree with someone's ideas or proposals, make sure you understand what you are agreeing *to* or *with*. There are long faces on many who did not get the true facts first.

If you find yourself impressed by others, and wish to offer support, be sure the Conduct impressing you is honorable and/or defendable. Taking sides in any discussion or conflict may require victory with force. Not everybody wins.

People sporting catchy, lofty titles in any arena are suspect and anyone associated with any alphabet agency is just plain dangerous. It is a sad state of affairs when you have to watch everyone and everything with both sets of eyes – front and back.

Be friendly, smile, trust few, and know that good people do good things, bad people do bad things, and an awful lot of people are aspiring and compromising liars.

Try to finish what you start and don't try to make any sense of another persons' Conduct. Keep in mind that a huge percentage of the general masses around you are boring, stupid slugs that do not deserve your attention. I refer to *this* as "paragraph eight (P8)" Conduct.

I mean no arrogance and try hard to be vigilant. Feel free to provide any conflicting *truth*.

Y'all take care now, ya' hear?!

ADDENDUM

When I first wrote this paper twenty-five years ago, our American "situation" was bad, but it did not occur to me how thoroughly the politicians would split and strip our wonderful country of any power, prestige and dignity, let alone Respect. When I re-wrote it in early 2013, I had been *well aware* of how the politicians were intentionally destroying our country. Presenting this document for publication forced me to realize that getting this message out was only part of the problem. Trying to articulate the level of damage, and what some of our options may be, became the other part.

To get started, I simply say that Barack Obama, as the great non-white hope, *blew it...* on purpose. What is so appalling is the fact that as the one person, who could have made the greatest positive changes in our country, and the world, chose to go the other way and consciously embark on a mission of hate, racism, division and destruction. He is doing an excellent job of destroying America and we have a lot of misery to prove it. He appears to be an *American Constitution*-hating Islamic who is supporting our enemies with money, arms and intelligence to press his seemingly pro-islam agenda. Worse, he has the bow and blessing of a wildly corrupt, *American Constitution*-hating criminal Congress to help him do his dirty work. Worse yet, he also has a blatantly corrupt and *American Constitution*-hating cabal of federal judges to give himself and his political associates backing and cover. Others have established his communist lineage and affiliation in detail. Let us also remember the complicit mainstream media.

Moreover, it appears that any ballot box hope is a pipe dream and it sure does look like Democrats are America-hating communist/islamics and Republicans are Democrats. That said, I could only assume that the cure for our political ills is a violent alternative. *We the people* are losing everything, and the bankers, politicians, judges, and three-fourths of the population are saying, "thank you." If any of the federal politicians had done just a little something within the constraints of the United States Constitution and the Bill of Rights, things might be a little different. With the NDAA (National Defense Authorization Act), and the NSA (National Security Agency), both being "secret standard" thugs, in full force; illegal no-knock, take-over, break-in, assault warrants now "*legal*;" and a corrupt bi-racial Kenyan of dubious origin in charge of the whole show, any *fair rules* are trashed. The corrupt politicos have enacted illegal laws and then selectively apply and enforce those laws. Meanwhile, they are holding themselves to seemingly NO standard. Now we have to start all over and work our way UP from the bottom. It looks to me as if the polarization between the people paying all the bills, and the people spending all the money, is very close to going *HOT.* Therefore – if someone positing some sort of authority shows up at your door, or stops you from traveling somewhere, it appears your choices are becoming horrible. Worse, true history proves that people who surrender guns end up in serious suffering and/or very dead. Like I said earlier, "Dig for the true facts. Otherwise, trust me. I already did the digging."

Conduct

Gosh Elmer, I wonder where the money comes from to pay all the bills, anyway?

Analyzing further, it sure looks like Obama is a "Manchurian Candidate" with NO authority to do ANYTHING (*The Manchurian Candidate*, 1959, by Richard Condon – A political thriller novel). Unfortunately, he had a lot of help getting where he is. His way to the White House was paved by massive corruption before him, and it sure does look as if the massive corruption will follow him. Lovely, isn't it? If you are alive fifty years hence, see what "history" you find in the public schools.

Just thinking here, but in trying to come up with the name of a couple of good presidents, I have to go back to the Founding Fathers era of this great nation. Most of the rest of the politicos are dirt bags... in my *opinion*, of course.

Standards, folks. With no appropriate standards and no *proper* enforcement, the pursuit and realization of real happiness is going dark... and let us be very clear on where those Standards *originally* came from. They are BIBLICAL, and all the Jew-Hating and Christian-Bashing gives us a good picture of what many people think of *STANDARDS*. Oh! Did you say you were not a Christian or a Jew and those standards do not apply to you? Well, well, well... I guess that makes it okay to kill you and beat, rape and/or kill the rest of your family! Hang around... isn't that the way islamics and their ilk handle it? Or worse...

Notice how we older Americans are polite and forgiving? Save it for your family and friends, then get over it! Times have changed dudes!

In closing, I can only say this, "If you don't have any *real* hair in the *right* place, you had best grow some." After you do that *growing*, you might want to do some rudimentary research about recent economic collapses and learn who suffers and who does not. It might cause you to grow something else... RESOLVE.

Oh, gosh... you did not know we are in an economic collapse? Hmmm... I guess those high prices for fewer goods are just Bad Luck. Stick around and see how soon your *Good* Luck arrives!

We are all finding out just how bad the politico Conspirators and their henchmen can make our lives. You might want a few things in preparation for the future –

> You *might* want a strong will to live with dignity...
> You *might* want a strong will to use the necessary tools...
> You *might* want a strong stomach for the storm, sights and smells surely coming.

My heart is breaking with the agony of knowledge... the knowledge of the recent past and near future, knowing it will be painful and messy. Frankly, I think we are going into "End Times." There is just too much malcontent, hate and mayhem around the world to ignore.

The Conspiracy – You will hear people tell you that any Conspiracy requires two or more people with some sort of plan, generally with suspicious motives, to keep a secret. The same talking heads blatting this crap will also tell you that the *government* and/or *industry*, cannot "keep" a secret. Oh, really?! Gee... I wonder why the wonderful folks trying to "blow the whistle" are persecuted and prosecuted with such focus, malice and vengeance?! I wonder why government and industry are working so hard to dumb down education and deny you access to any information about *their* Conduct?! How about inflation and all the magnificent financial losses of so many people? "They" are all working overtime, in secret, to screw you! Bottom line - You cannot challenge something of which you are not aware.

The Corruption – This subject is so vast, and so astonishing, it is unbelievable to most people. If non-caring Americans had any idea of how horribly they are being treated and manipulated for a deplorable future, they would probably deny it and defend that denial. Oh! Wait a minute! Here it is right on your doorstep, and since the Komrades on TV did not say anything, "it" doesn't exist, right?! Brother... if you only knew where a lot of that so-called *Foreign Aid* really goes... Hey, if you need a little amusement, try following all the money in local government. Good luck getting the proper, complete and truthful information. You will likely find these problems in any inquiry, anywhere. Bummer...

I wonder how many people receiving government handouts would vote for, or even care about, any necessary change for the benefit of restoring our Republic? I know, I know, it is a stupid question. Good grief... It's a joke, pal...

The Courage – This is where your butt hits the burr - hard. This is where you have an epiphany and wake up to the realization of all the trouble intentionally put upon you. This is where the wall of denial and deception, the will to get the true facts, and the seemingly impossible ability to "do" something, all converge to give you the attitude, resolve, and strength to make a change. Now it is time to make your own situation and future go where YOU want it to go. This is the point of no return, where you now realize that crying, complaining, and seeking comfort in the company of other whiners and complainers is a go-nowhere, do-nothing dead end.

It is confrontation time, folks. Life can be hell and it is time to forget the past, scrap the petty emotional attachments, and forge through to the future. With all the human garbage willfully making your life difficult, you must crush… and keep crushing. Make an example of someone or something that incontrovertibly proves you are serious.

If bad people need to go to hell, make it worth your while. Do not waste too much time on any tears… the situation at hand will need your undivided attention and likely outlive you. Remember – the present and future are products of the past. Someone, somewhere… or you… *caused* it.

The OTHER Golden Rule – With homegrown political ideology that allows and facilitates death, destruction and misery of all kinds and types – the time may be here for the *other* Golden Rule – *Do unto them as they most certainly plan on doing unto you*! When was the last time you saw any good guys in conflict who sat around and watched the enemy launch a rocket at them? I will bet you would hang around to see if the enemy can aim… am I right?! Smile, dude.

Maybe the last little portion of my paper seems a tad presumptuous. Nevertheless… on my way to Heaven, I might have to show some charity and help a few devils back to hell. After all, I am not much good to anybody, or any cause, if I am starving, maimed or dead. Is that Good Conduct??

I hope you have a wonderful and prosperous future to enjoy for a long time… with plenty of that Good Conduct!

MYSELF – YOUR AUTHOR

As the son of loving parents who led busy lives in science, industry and faith, I have been provided with a life having strong foundations and expectations.

In the mid-1960's I enlisted in the United States Marine Corps and would go on to duty in the Viet Nam War, earning various decorations and citations in the combat zone. Something else happened too... I started asking others and myself how the U.S. could do such a lousy job of **Conducting** a war. I found that the deeper I dug, the more frustrated I became. I decided to start making short speeches to vent my ideas. As my base of associates grew, and my knowledge broadened, I knew some sort of a book was in my future. I did not know it would be another 30 years.

Good luck has been with me and I have enjoyed employment in numerous capacities throughout industry, manufacturing, and commerce. Having been led to several opportunities, I paid close attention to the industrial "hierarchy" making many memories and noting the actions and reactions of various players.

A defining moment was an introduction to Oscar R. Dudley, a retired Texas flying geologist from whom I would learn and work with in the oil field. This would lead me to a Texas Oilman who would invest time and money in me, providing education and experience related to drilling, mining and more. Later, in Colorado, I started my own oil company, which included a mixed bag of good and bad luck.

The Colorado Company "ran its course," and I returned to Ohio where I joined local industry. By early 2003, both parents had passed, the "nine-eleven" twin-tower assault had happened, and my employment stopped when the company closed. By this time, I had been studying political and economic trends and realized that a lot of the bad luck people were having was because someone else caused it. It was time to finish outlining my book.

Having seen plenty of difficulty in life, I learned how sickness, death, bad Conduct and flattened bank accounts can happen and screw up good people. Others know it too, and we are not first or alone in anything, anywhere.

I stay busy with various projects and hobbies. One of those hobbies is trying to make people aware of some of the political dynamics that shape their lives… dynamics so huge and bizarre they seem unbelievable. I think of this as a game I might win someday.

Stay safe…

****

Happiness is free. Keep plenty on hand for everyone

****

Miscellany

USMC – Combat Air Crew; Air & Ground Electronics

Colorado School of Mines – Uranium Geology

New Mexico Institute of Mining and Technology – Uranium Geology

The Institute for Energy Development (OK) – Oil & Gas Contracts; Petroleum Land Titles

Arizona State University – Vegetable Oil for Industrial Applications

Lethal Force Institute – Use of Deadly Force for Private Citizens

Tactical Defense Institute – Level I, II & III Handgun Training

Various Colleges – Literature; Math; Engineering; etc.

Other Schools – Union Management Relations; Gunsmith; Investigations and more

Mining, Drilling, Manufacturing, Industry & Commerce – 30 years

Proprietor – Gas Station, Garage, Gun Store

Landlord – 30 years